CAMBRIDGE ANGLO-NORMAN TEXTS

General Editor:
O. H. PRIOR, M.A., D. ès L.
Drapers Professor of French

CAMBRIDGE ANGLO-NORMAN TEXTS

POEM ON THE ASSUMPTION
Edited by J. P. STRACHEY, *Principal of Newnham College*

POEM ON THE DAY OF JUDGMENT
Edited by H. J. CHAYTOR, *Fellow of St Catharine's College*

DIVISIONES MUNDI
Edited by O. H. PRIOR, *Fellow of St John's College*

CAMBRIDGE
AT THE UNIVERSITY PRESS
1924

CAMBRIDGE UNIVERSITY PRESS
Cambridge, New York, Melbourne, Madrid, Cape Town,
Singapore, São Paulo, Delhi, Tokyo, Mexico City

Cambridge University Press
The Edinburgh Building, Cambridge CB2 8RU, UK

Published in the United States of America by Cambridge University Press, New York

www.cambridge.org
Information on this title: www.cambridge.org/9781107600553

First published 1924
First paperback edition 2011

A catalogue record for this publication is available from the British Library

ISBN 978-1-107-60055-3 Paperback

CONTENTS

PREFACE

WITH this volume, the Cambridge Anglo-Norman
Society is endeavouring to justify its existence. Its
first effort is obviously tentative and is drawn up on experi-
mental lines. The works selected are representative of three
genres, a purely didactic poem on Geography, a legend of
the Virgin, and a biblical subject. All these are necessarily
short, as are the notes and the preface: our excuse is that
we are strictly limited for space. We have to thank the
Syndics of the University Press for kindly undertaking the
publication of this, our first volume. But they were naturally
not inclined to allow unlimited space for a subject which can
appeal only to comparatively few.

Still, the plan of the Society is sufficiently comprehensive,
and its productions ought to be of use and interest to a wider
public than the mere student of Anglo-Norman. Our purpose
is to edit the numerous manuscripts which are to be found in
the Cambridge University and College libraries. We are by
no means bound down to purely literary work, but propose to
include in our series documents of interest from social, economic,
political, legal points of view. Many such have already been
edited by History specialists in particular, but experience
has proved that linguistic, philological knowledge is essential
if such documents are to prove valuable as sources. It is owing
to the repeated complaints of scholars in other branches that we
have decided thus to widen the scope of our undertaking. We
hope that a combined effort between Anglo-Norman specialists
and others will produce the best results, and the first step in
that direction has been taken by our legal friends whose plan
for an edition of Anglo-Norman documents coincides with
ours.

But political, legal and literary documents are obvious
matter for editing. There is more than that to be found in our
libraries: medical and culinary recipes, fragments of all sorts and
descriptions offer new and almost untouched material to the
student of economics and of medieval customs in England.
One of our members has undertaken the collation of Anglo-
Norman proverbs which may serve to illustrate our ancestors'
peculiar turn of mind. The material for such research lies

scattered in many manuscripts, very often too in the bindings of old works, a fact well known to all collectors and book lovers.

We have a further aim in thus widening the range of our subjects: only a wealth of documents will allow us to solve, by means of an accumulation of material, the many problems presented by Anglo-Norman.

It is the general editor's purpose to discuss in the next few pages some of these problems and the solutions which can be offered. But he takes full responsibility for views and theories propounded here which are not held by all scholars, not even necessarily by all members of the Cambridge Anglo-Norman Society. They embody the result of many years' study of Anglo-Norman documents in England as well as abroad.

*   *   *

If a definition is needed of what is meant by Anglo-Norman, I may say briefly that this name denotes that form of the French language which was spoken and written in England and Ireland from the Conquest until the end of the fourteenth century. On that point scholars agree; but some insist on calling this language Anglo-French, others divide the whole period into two parts, and call one Anglo-Norman and the other Anglo-French. For reasons which will become evident later, I use throughout this Preface the term Anglo-Norman.

Considerations of space allow me here to refer only to the chief and more recent works on the subject of Anglo-Norman, works in which, frequently, full bibliographies are to be found, and where older theories are discussed and new ones propounded. I thus mention especially:

L. E. Menger. *The Anglo-Norman Dialect.* (Columbia University Press, 1904.)
A. Stimming. *Der anglonormannische Boeve de Haumtone.* (Halle, 1899.)
P. Studer. *The Study of Anglo-Norman.* (Oxford, 1920.)
H. Suchier. *Ueber die Matthaeus Paris zugeschriebene Vie de Seint Auban.* (Halle, 1876.)
—— *Altfranzösische Grammatik.* (Halle, 1893.)
F. J. Tanquerey. *L'évolution du verbe en anglo-français.* (Paris, 1915.)
—— *Recueil de Lettres anglo-françaises.* (Paris, 1916.)
—— *Plaintes de la Vierge.* (Paris, 1921.)
J. Vising. *Anglo-Norman Language and Literature.* (Oxford University Press, 1923.)

*   *   *

There is now-a-days an apparently overwhelming body of opinion in favour of the theory that Norman influence was preponderant in England after the Conquest. According to

many authorities, native customs, arts, literature, nay the very
language vanished before the combined forces of a superior
civilisation and a multitude of invaders. The arguments of such
critics are numerous and apparently convincing. They can quote
the undeniable political and literary superiority of the Norman
conquerors; they can prove the fact that French alone was
spoken at Court, in the Schools, in the law-courts. Poets, prose-
writers used hardly any other language except that of the conquerors. There were not only Norman settlers in England:
political circumstances brought into the country, at various
times, Flemings, Walloons, Provençals. The greater part of the
higher clergy came from abroad. English as a language almost
seemed to vanish; and our native writers, during the twelfth
century at least, were but the feeble heirs of Old English literary
giants.

And yet, this Norman poetry which is supposed to be the
only medium of expression of native genius has strange features
of its own, very different from those of the Continent. Our poets
write their verses in French, it is true, but their rhythm is unusual
and their lines are sometimes too short, sometimes too long. A
rash critic has even asserted that our ancestors, through sheer
ignorance or carelessness, were unable to count syllables up to
ten, and that thus their epic lines had nine or even eleven
syllables.

For more than three centuries, it would seem, our poets lost
all sense of rhythm, and followed no laws. Obviously such an
opinion is absurd, and I shall not be the first to endeavour to
prove that French poetry in England is based on a well defined
rhythm, not borrowed from abroad but of spontaneous and
native growth.

But if this new rhythm seems odd to Continental ears, the
French language itself, as spoken in England, is equally strange.
It undergoes, from the time of the Conquest, a separate process
of evolution which affects both the morphology and the
phonetics. Here again, our critics seem to see no method in
the changes: Anglo-Normans, they say, merely use one vowel
for another, develop, without rhyme or reason, new diphthongs
and consonants, or borrow sounds from all invaders alike:
Walloons, Flemings and others.

Meanwhile we find that the native, the English, dialects are
changing in a perfectly consistent and normal manner. The
process has not yet been studied in all its details, but one fact
stands out strikingly: the evolution of sounds in English is,
in many respects, closely akin to that of the French language

in England. And thus I venture to draw from this the following conclusion: the phonetic evolution of Anglo-Norman is similar to, if not entirely dependent on, that of Middle English dialects.

This amounts to a negation of Norman and other Continental influences. Logically it should lead to a discussion of the two well-known theses of Celtic versus Germanic influences. This is not merely a matter of Philology: it implies a revision of the whole question of British Ethnology; it is obviously outside the scope of this preface and I can only venture here on a few general remarks.

*   *   *

The state of England at the time of the Conquest may be described approximately as follows. The population had become more or less blended into one race; its ethnological characteristics were well defined; its habits and customs were original. Arts and literature were flourishing. The language itself, with its sonorous vowels, its varied inflections, was well adapted to a system of poetry, the rhythm of which was based on accented syllables and alliterations. But in the eleventh century, both the literary language and the rhythm seem to have been checked in their development: the poets no longer speak or write for the people. The old vocalic system is progressing; the morphology is simplified by the loss of inflections: but poetry does not follow this evolution and maintains the old linguistic features.

This peculiar state of poetry seems to have been completely altered by the Conquest: English ceased for a long time to be a literary medium, and writers who did not use the clerks' language, Latin, were forced by circumstances to use Norman-French. Hence the disappearance of the old poetic tradition: the pre-Conquest system could not find favour with the new Court; it was out of touch with the people. And thus when Layamon strove, for the first time, to write a poem in the native language, he had to overcome almost insuperable difficulties. We see the result of his efforts to find a new rhythm, a combination of accents and alliterations, in his *Brut*. The change from alliteration to an accentual system can be followed even more closely in the *Proverbs* of Alfred.

This evolution may seem at first sight rather sudden, but it can be readily accounted for: since the loss of the old phonetic and inflectional system alliteration no longer satisfied the requirements of English rhythm. The Conquest brought to a by no means untimely end the antiquated and artificial poetry of

English bards. The new poetry, written for the people, set aside all the obsolete forms, and adopted the contemporary language and inflections. But it required also a new rhythm. The native poets had to choose between two systems which were even then in constant use in England itself: the syllabic system of the Normans, the accentual system of Latin rhythmic verse, already adopted by, or perhaps even natural to, the Celts. This alternative explains doubtless the hesitations of Layamon and our Early Middle English writers.

The difficulty was settled by the very nature of the English language. Throughout its history, one feature has persisted from the earliest days to our own times: the stress or accent which, in every word, marks a tonic syllable. This stress is not necessarily, as in Germanic languages, permanently fixed on the root-syllable of the word; there is rather a tendency to carry it back to the first syllable, thus giving to the English language a suppleness and a variety unknown in other Northern tongues. We notice, in every linguistic group, one permanent and invariable feature which may serve to distinguish it from another: namely, the system of accents. Romance languages have one of their own, Germanic languages another, English yet a different one. Thus our poets adopted a rhythm corresponding to the mode of stressing which was natural to them. The Norman syllabic system was used in a few exceptional cases of comparatively little importance, but on the whole neither the French nor the Germanic rhythm ever succeeded in taking root in England.

We have here, it seems to me, a very strong argument in favour of English ethnological unity, after, as well as before, the Conquest. This unity and racial originality stand out in many other directions. English poetry has always had distinctive features of its own; the same remark applies to music: the North developed, in singing, a style peculiar to itself, which is described by Giraldus Cambrensis; our carols, the polyphonic *Summer is icumen in* of MS. Harley 948, all rank amongst the most original productions of the Middle Ages. Architecture in England was not a mere slavish imitation of Continental schools: churches, castles, houses, all possess special features unknown elsewhere. Our architects and masons have left traces of their work on the Continent, where they were employed and appreciated on account of their skill.

The artistic temperament of the English showed itself in many other directions. No one can fail to recognize and admire English manuscripts illuminated by our scribes: their art may have been equalled by other schools; it has not been surpassed. It was in demand everywhere in the thirteenth century, and was at its best towards the end of that period. Equally renowned was the embroidery known as *opus anglicanum*. Add to this the carving of statues, the book-bindings of London, Winchester and Durham, enamel, stained glass: in all these branches English artists were noted for their beautiful colourings, for the originality of their designs, for their craftsmanship.

In his *Dictionnaire d'orfèvrerie*, the abbé Tessier gives a list of English goldsmiths which goes back to the Saxon period. Matthew Paris describes in laudatory terms their remarkable works, which were found even in Rome, in St Peter's. The reliquary of St Thomas of Canterbury was known as the finest in Christendom. Unfortunately only a few examples of this kind of work have come down to us, but what we possess suffices to show an extraordinarily high level of excellence. Repeatedly French inventories contain such entries as "a silver box, the work of an Englishman," "a gold cup, enamelled in England," "a salt-cellar of English workmanship." A really complete and comprehensive work on the subject of art in Early England has yet to be written; but the materials for such a work are plentiful, and even now what we know on the subject is enough to prove the originality of our artists before, as well as after, the Conquest.

Originality in language, in accentuation, in rhythm, in arts and crafts, all these arguments seem to emphasize the fact that the Norman invasion had far less influence on the development of our race than is generally supposed. This influence is undeniable in politics and in law; but in other respects it has been much exaggerated. In other countries where they settled, in France, in Sicily, the Normans, as a race, showed very little power of resistance to the native element. There is no cogent reason why they should have proved more refractory in England.

The numbers of the invaders do not seem to have been overwhelming[1]. They formed a minority in the midst of a population which historians estimate at over two million souls. The latest analysis of Domesday Book confirms this figure, which is of course still approximate. But calculations based on the feeding capacity of the country and the amount of land

---

[1] Hill, quoted by Vising, estimates the number of Frenchmen who settled in England during the Conqueror's reign at about 200,000. This figure seems to be much exaggerated. (Cf. G. Hill, *Some consequences of the Norman Conquest*, London, 1904.—Vising, *o.c.*, p. 9.)

under cultivation will certainly bring us nearer to the truth
and help to solve the problem. The vague and contradictory
information given on this subject by Chroniclers is of doubtful value.

We can hardly take into account that floating population
of merchants and journeymen, the same in all countries,
which leaves traces in the vocabulary, in the form of technical
terms for instance, but which does not affect the great national
strata. Thus Jews settled in large numbers in England. But
we have here a curious instance of the power of English culture
to assimilate a foreign element. Jews who crossed the Channel
immediately after the Conquest bore mostly French names,
" Bon Enfaunt," " Deu-le-Garde," "Le Chanteur"; but a Jew,
living in England and born at the latest in 1235, calls himself
" Bullok," another " Biscop," etc. Obviously they found it to
their advantage to adapt themselves to their surroundings.

After 1066, the nobility was mostly composed of Normans,
although William wisely respected the rights of some of the old
English families. But very soon intermarriages between the two
races became numerous, and we have every reason to believe
that here as elsewhere the mother's speech and influence pre-
vailed. French remained the official language of the Court, but
there is no proof that the families of the nobility itself generally
used the conquerors' language as a medium. If they spoke
French at all it was of the kind described by Chaucer as
" French of Stratford-at-Bow ": witness the humorous references to the jargon of our English noblemen or others in many
French works from the thirteenth century onwards. In fact
French was learnt as a foreign language, and we still possess
Biblesworth's vocabulary, written for the purpose of teaching
French to the noble family of Mounchensy. The vast number
of copies of this work which have come down to us suffice to
show that it answered a definite and fairly widespread need
of the times. Thus the children of the Norman ruling class
learnt French, or rather Anglo-Norman, through the medium
of English; and this accounts for the numerous treatises on
hunting, heraldry, etc., written in Anglo-Norman obviously
for the use of the aristocracy.

The higher clergy, as in the rest of Europe, was selected
irrespective of nationality. Bishoprics, benefices of all kinds
were in the hands of Italians, Frenchmen, Swiss, Germans.
But from the beginning the English preferred their native
clergy, and St Thomas of Canterbury owed his popularity
partly to his British descent or associations. Several foreign

bishops found it necessary to learn *English* in order to be understood by the people.

The lower clergy was chiefly drawn from the native English population and maintained its peculiar institutions against foreign intervention. Thus the marriage of priests is a common practice even in the twelfth century.

Woman must have been the chief factor in this resistance of English elements to Norman penetration. Ordericus Vitalis, born in England of a Norman father and an English mother, learns French in Normandy and is proud to call himself English. This seems to have been, in general, the fate of the conquerors: they settled in England, married native women; their children spoke the mother's language, and within one generation they became English.

How are we to explain that for more than two centuries the language of England, both spoken and literary, is Anglo-Norman and not English, if we admit that the population was English and the Norman admixture comparatively insignificant? To my mind, this preponderance of Anglo-Norman is fictitious: French, in England, has always been a *lingua adventitia*, as Ranulph Higden calls it. It is quite probable that William understood the value of language as a means of penetration and ruling. He encouraged French culture by all possible means and especially by the most powerful of all, by means of education.

Historians have not laid sufficient stress on this very important side of Norman action. In medieval England there seems to have been a general taste for learning, and records are there to show that means of education were plentiful in the country as well as in the towns. In the Eastern counties, for instance, in Norfolk and Lincolnshire there were at least as many schools in the Middle Ages as there are now. In London alone there were four. Many villages or country towns, such as Dunstable, have left a mark in our educational history, though we hardly hear of them now in that connection.

The studies were obviously of an elementary character, but they attracted people from the lower as well as the middle classes who found in them a means of rising in the world by becoming clerks, merchants, etc. In the schools, English as a medium of instruction was banned. The languages used were Latin and French: this was a feature peculiar to England. Statutes show us a similar state of affairs in the Universities; students are forbidden to talk to one another except in Latin or French. If such regulations were necessary, do we need a better proof that English must have been spoken by the majority? Clearly French was the literary language, the language of the Court: for this reason Trevisa, describing the people of the middle classes and even the peasants, says that when they wish to be genteel they try to speak French.

The clergy, clerks and others, compelled to teach in a foreign language and yet seldom in touch with the Continent, soon lost their grip of standard French. Native expressions and constructions, the English accent itself, were bound to influence the foreign idiom. And thus was gradually evolved the dialect which we know by the name of Anglo-Norman, a form of French strongly influenced by English, never spoken by the people, but purely an instrument of teaching: a *lingua adventitia*. We now understand the foreign gibes at "English French," Chaucer's allusion to the French of Stratford-at-Bow, and, earlier still, Walter Mapes' reference to the "spring" at Marlborough. Anyone who drinks of it, he says, *Gallice barbarizat*. Thus, as early as the twelfth century, school-French was notorious. For there is little doubt that Walter Mapes' allusion to the "spring" refers to the "fountain of knowledge," namely the School of Marlborough which is mentioned in a document dated 1232[1].

This special use of French for didactic purposes further explains the existence of a vast Anglo-Norman literature of a purely technical character which has come down to us: works on geography, history, saints' lives, etc.; all these formed the material for reading or teaching in schools[2].

And thus we come back to our original argument: Anglo-

---

[1] Cf. A. F. Leach, *Educational Charters* (Cambridge, 1911), p. 152: "Gregorius episcopus...Magistro Scolarum de Merleberge, Saresberiensis diocesis, salutem...."

[2] I may here suggest that the subject of the origins of our theatre is intimately related to this question of teaching. Chambers and others find in an Anglo-Norman theatre, which has been lost, the origin of our English mystery and miracle plays. This was certainly not a subject of teaching in schools and the earlier plays were surely written in Latin and not in French. When the theatre became *popular* and the *people* themselves took part in acting, French would have been even more out of place: an audience of English-speaking people would not have derived much amusement from plays acted in a foreign tongue, and the moral or religious value of the mystery would have been problematic. The question however is still obscure: but, pending further proofs, I can hardly believe in the Norman origins of the English stage. The earliest example of a mystery in French, the *Jeu d'Adam*, is Norman far more than Anglo-Norman. The oft quoted *Ludus de Sancta Katerina* was written by a French schoolmaster at Dunstable, but the text was probably Latin. There is no proof in favour of French. (Cf. A. F. Leach, *o.c.* p. 78, *St Albans and Dunstable Schools in the 12th century*: "Gaufridus...de Cenomannia...quemdam ludum de Sancta Katerina, quem Miracula vulgariter appellamus, fecit.")

Norman was a purely artificial language forced upon an English population for political purposes by the Conqueror.

When French ceased to be taught in schools, its importance vanished at once. If we are to believe Trevisa, this event happened in the year 1385 and was the work of John Cornwall, schoolmaster, who can thus be considered as, indirectly, the father of English literature, and the source of English patriotism[1]. The old Norman tradition was maintained, however, by lawyers, and up to modern times, a strange jargon, quite unlike French, or even Anglo-Norman, has been used under the name of "law-French," a living proof of the importance attached to the use of their language by the Norman rulers. To this group of works belong such documents as the "Oak-book" of Southampton. The forms of oath which they contained were compulsory on everybody, but an Englishman taking such an oath probably did not understand its French any more than he would the Latin formulae required in other cases.

The use of French then was obligatory in schools, but the mere pressure of the native English culture and language brought about, in the foreign idiom, fundamental changes which the Norman rulers had no power to prevent. A few years after the Conquest we notice the first signs of this English reaction: morphology, syntax, stress-accent on words, rhythm, phonetics, this is, very approximately and broadly, the chronological order of the decay of Norman French. I use the word "decay" here with many reservations, for it hardly seems to fit the case of Anglo-Norman which, as I shall endeavour to show later, merely follows the evolution of English dialects.

This phonetic influence of English can be traced further in the formation of Anglo-Norman rhythm: Norman poetry gradually ceased to be syllabic and became accentual. There was little difficulty in such a change, for French polysyllables, owing to the natural English tendency to carry the accent as far back as possible, could be stressed according to the poet's fancy. Thus in Chaucer words of French origin vary in their accentuation and we find "hónour" as well as "honoúr."

It is quite possible that even the earliest poems in Anglo-Norman were composed in rhythmic verses: they are still strictly syllabic, but can be read without difficulty as iambics.

---

[1] "For John Cornwaile, a maister of Grammer, chaunged the lore in gramer scole and construccioun of Frensche in to Englische...so that now, the yere of our Lorde a thowsand thre hundred and foure score and five...in alle the gramere scoles of Engelond, children leue Frensche and construe and lerne an Englishe...."
(In Trevisa's translation of Higden's *Polychronicon*.)

But later, when the lines become irregular, when they are too long or too short according to the French system, we cannot scan them otherwise than by stresses. These verses are only too often described by critics as faulty; editors endeavour to "correct" them by adding syllables in some cases, eliding them in others, by altering words or sentences, though the meaning may be perfectly clear without any such emendations.

Anglo-Norman poems have all the well-known characteristics of English rhythm: monosyllables are stressed or not, at will; polysyllables bear the accent on the first, second or third syllable; a word of four syllables, or more, may have two accents; two consecutive syllables may remain unstressed; an *e* mute before another vowel is sometimes elided, sometimes not. A so-called Norman line of eight syllables might thus have only seven syllables in Anglo-Norman if it happened to be a catalectic line with four stress accents.

I now select a few examples, taken chiefly from Schipper and Saintsbury's works[1], to illustrate some of the characteristic features of Middle English prosody.

Normal line with four stressed syllables corresponding to the French eight-syllable line:

> Nou shrínkeþ róse and lýlie floúr.

Catalectic line with four accents (seven syllables instead of eight):

> Gíf we leórniþ Gódes láre (*Pater Noster*).

Five-stress line with unstressed syllable omitted before the caesura (French heroic line with nine syllables instead of ten):

> Enhástyng hím, | tíl he wás at lárge (Lydgate, *Story of Thebes*).

Line with accent on a normally unstressed syllable:

> For whý this ís more thén that caúse ís (Chaucer, *House of Fame*).

Line in which a dissyllabic word bears the stress on the unaccented syllable:

> Of clóth makýng | she hádde súch an haúnt (Chaucer, *Prologue*).

In the following example, an unaccented syllable has been omitted in the body of the line:

> Hálde wé Gódes láȝe (*Pater Noster*).

This line being catalectic, two unaccented syllables are omitted. Thus a normal line of eight syllables is reduced to six, without in any way impairing the rhythm of the verse.

The contrary process is seen in the following line where the first unaccented syllable in an iambic foot is preceded by

[1] J. Schipper, *A History of English Versification* (Oxford, 1910); G. Saintsbury, *A History of English Prosody* (2 vols., London, 1910).

another syllable similarly unaccented, thus producing a line of *nine* syllables instead of *eight*:

> Gif we clépieþ híne féder þénne (*Pater Noster*).

This is a poetic licence common even in Modern English, as for instance in the well-known line of Coleridge:

> By thy lóng grey beárd and glíttering éye.

This additional unstressed syllable occurs also in the body of the line:

> In Wéssex was thán a Kíng, | his náme wás Sir Íne (Rob. Manning).

Thus, in some cases, the rhythmic accent is alone considered, and both the tonic and the syntactical accents are ignored. Such is the case in the lines which begin "Of cloth makyng..." and "For why this is more...." There is little aesthetic feeling in such licences; they are perhaps less objectionable than elsewhere in didactic poems in which technical perfection is not the primary object: hence doubtless their frequent occurrence in Anglo-Norman literature.

Further, in Middle English, the rules as to the use or elision of an unstressed *e* in the body or at the end of a word are numerous and seemingly very elastic. Broadly speaking, a final *e* is elided before another vowel, and frequently too before a consonant. The following example occurs in the *Moral Ode*:

> And þá, þe úntreownéss(e) dide þán.

All the above lines illustrate only a few of the original features of Middle English poetry, but they suffice to show that such licences were natural to it. Thus our poets merely applied their native rhythm to French verse when they wrote lines of seven instead of eight, eleven instead of ten syllables.

The importance of the accent in Anglo-Norman verse explains other developments equally characteristic of this poetry: the line now forms a rhythmic unit easily realized by the ear; hence the *rhyme* loses its paramount importance, and the rules which govern its use are much relaxed. Thus we find the same sound used in several consecutive couplets; the poet's ear is satisfied with mere assonance; a word can rhyme with itself; and lastly the sentence frequently extends not only beyond the line, but even beyond the couplet or stanza.

The adaptation of English rhythm to French poetry had a further result, well known to readers of Middle English literature: in the same verse we often find a mixture of two or even three languages, one line being written in English, another in Latin and a third in French. It is worthy of note that those same authors who are accused of ignorance in the matter of

Anglo-Norman metre, manage to write excellent rhythmic verse in both Latin and English.

Here is an example of Anglo-Norman and Latin lines joined in one couplet:

Dum lúdis flóribús, velút lacíniá,
Le diéu d'amoúr moi tiént en tiél angústiá[1].

One of the most interesting and graceful examples of this *genre* is a prayer to the Virgin in six verses, of which this is the first:

Maíden móder mílde
Oiéz cel óreysoún
From sháme þoú me shílde
E dé ly málfeloún.
For lóue of þíne chílde
Me ménez dé tresoún.
Ích wes wód and wílde;
Óre su én prisoún.

It should be evident now that our poets wrote French verses according to their own rhythmic system: but it is also evident that the usual French terminology is misleading in this case. We ought not to describe Anglo-Norman lines as decasyllabic, but as lines with five stresses. Octosyllabic verse is really four-stressed, etc.

This new system of versification produced another feature, well known to editors of Anglo-Norman texts. For an obvious reason the various MSS. of a poem differ far more in Anglo-Norman than they do in French, for, with the various licences permissible in Anglo-Norman poetry, it is by no means always clear how the author of any given poem places his accents; hence many difficulties, quite unknown to French poets and scribes, which readily explain the numerous alternative readings. Prose manuscripts, on the other hand, agree far more closely, as the question of accents does not arise. Having allowed for differences of rhythm, we are bound to admit that another element of error affects Anglo-Norman manuscripts more than others: our scribes wrote in a foreign tongue, and traces of imperfect knowledge are often very evident.

The editor of an Anglo-Norman poem has before him a very delicate and difficult task, for he has to take into consideration many points which seldom arise in the case of Continental MSS.

The following lines are taken from the poem of Benoît de St Albans on St Thomas of Canterbury. It dates from the

---

[1] These lines are taken from the British Museum MS. Harley 2253 (end of thirteenth century and beginning of fourteenth).

beginning of the thirteenth century and contains many of the so-called "licences" of English poetry. The rhythm is evidently iambic[1].

> Al De*ú* | lo*é*nge | en s*ó*n | serv*í*s,
> P*á*r | la gr*á*ce | que m'*á*d | tram*í*s
> D*é* | chant*é*r
> D*é* | cel*uí* | qui s*á*nz | feint*í*se
> Se c*ó*m|bat*í* | pur se*í*nt | Esgl*í*se
> *A*|vanc*é*r;
> Ceo *é*st | l'ercev*é*s|que se*í*nt | Thom*á*s
> Qui d*é* | cler s*á*nc | ot te*í*nt | ces dr*á*s
> Pur De*ú* | am*ú*r;
> Et c'*í*l | se f*í*t | hombl*é*s | et b*á*s,
> Mart*í*r | en f*é*t | pur *ú*n | tresp*á*s
> A gr*á*nt | hon*ú*r.
>
> (Ed. F. Michel, *Chronique*, III, p. 461.)

*   *   *

We now pass on to another important factor in the evolution of Anglo-Norman: the influence of English dialects which affect the phonetics and spelling of author and scribe alike. This is the part of my subject for which material is most scanty. I am here on very debatable ground and readily admit that definite results can only be attained by means of intelligent co-operation between students of English dialects and of Anglo-Norman.

The present difficulty is due especially to a lack of materials and of any standard work entirely devoted to early dialects, such as we find in France. Monographs, doctor's theses are numerous, but they are far from solving all the problems. The comparative dearth of Middle English texts of the twelfth and thirteenth centuries is an obstacle; but still we possess in our libraries and Record offices much material which will prove useful. A careful study of such documents is the only safe introduction to a complete knowledge of English dialects. There is nothing in England which can be compared to Gilliéron's *Atlas*, and our modern dialects are insufficiently known. Wright's *Dialect Dictionary* and his *Grammar*[2] provide most valuable material, but it is evident that some of Wright's collaborators lacked phonetic training and many conclusions are open to question. Still, the harvest gathered by Wright is rich enough to help us to settle many points.

Suchier[3] was the first to classify Anglo-Norman manuscripts from a geographical and historical point of view according to

---

[1] I have marked in this case not only the stresses but also the feet.
[2] J. Wright, *The English Dialect Grammar* (Oxford, 1905).
[3] Cf. Suchier's *Altfranzösische Grammatik* and his *Vie de Seint Auban*.

certain characteristic features. Thus the use or absence of the rhyme u ($<$ L. ū) : u ($<$ L. ō)[1] distinguished, according to him, works written in the North of England from those of the South; for this is a rhyme unknown in French but quite possible in the North of England, where there was confusion between o and u. As regards time, Suchier divided Anglo-Norman into periods, each of which had phonetic features of its own. M. Tanquerey, in his study on the verb in Anglo-Norman, selects for his historical dates 1110, 1160 and 1250, and his conclusions are based on very sound arguments. But he insists perhaps too much on Walloon influences which, according to him, appear in Anglo-Norman in or about 1250. I have already stated the reasons which render this hypothesis doubtful, especially from an ethnological point of view.

But it is only by discussing conclusions of this kind that we may hope to arrive at definite results.

Thus the formation of diphthongs is certainly one of the phenomena which distinguish Walloon from other dialects. But we find a parallel to this in England itself, and reference to foreign and therefore more distant and problematic influences is unnecessary. In fact diphthongization is one of the chief features of Middle English phonetics. The origins of this phenomenon can be traced to the pre-Conquest period : no French or Continental influence can be claimed in this case. There is nothing improbable, to say the least, in my assumption that the forces, whatever they may be, which brought about the division of vowels in English acted in a similar way on French vowels as pronounced in England. In Middle English, i diphthongs such as ai, ei are found everywhere, while ie occurs in dialects. This may well account for the formation of similar i diphthongs in Anglo-Norman.

As an instance of the varied evolution of Old English sounds, we may take the long vowel $\overline{eo}$, which gave in general ee in Middle English, but ie in Kent, ue in the South-West (O.E. *deop* > M.E. *deep*, Kent *diep*, S.W. *duep*).

Such dialectal differences were noticed even by our early authors. Trevisa states that the people of the South can hardly understand those from the North. Caxton[2] relates the story of a merchant whom a Yorkshire woman took for a Frenchman because he asked for *eggys* instead of *eyren*. *And the merchant was angry*, adds Caxton, *for he also could speke no frensche*. We may draw from this anecdote the additional

[1] e.g. hure ($<$ L. horam) : nature.
[2] Prologue to *Aeneid*.

inference that it was possible for an English merchant to trade without knowing French, and this in spite of Norman or Latin oaths.

Now a study of the origin of our Middle English diphthongs will bring out one important fact: the source is purely English and the evolution, in each case, is quite normal and free from foreign elements. The only diphthong obviously borrowed from the French is *oi*, and this is seldom found except in loanwords such as *joie, coi, oyster, exploit*, etc.

On the other hand, French loan-words in Middle English receive a strong stress-accent on the model of English words, and their vocalic scheme is from the very first adapted to the English: for, even in the twelfth century, loan-words of French origin rhyme with native words, unless of course the rhyme is in *oi*[1].

an, aun.

French nasal sounds vanished entirely, nasals being unknown to Middle English. In this connection I have to discuss the phonetic value of *an*, which has given rise to several theories and is even held as a proof of the existence of at least one nasal sound in English. During a certain period, Anglo-Norman scribes spelt this sound *aun*, a spelling which has survived in many English words to this day.

The French *an* has produced in Modern English sometimes [ɔn], sometimes [ɑn]. Wyld attributes this difference to social causes. According to his theory the *Court* and the *higher classes* spoke with a French accent and preserved a nasal pronunciation of *an* of which, however, they made a diphthong, *aun*. *aun*, later, became [ɔn] as we find it in, e.g., *to haunt*. But in French words borrowed by the *people*, *an* did not become a diphthong and merely lost its nasal value. Hence such words as *branch, dance*, etc.

I venture to suggest that this phonetic selection between Court words and popular words is improbable, none of those words being of a technical nature such as would restrict their use to the Court or higher classes. It is rather a question of chronology and dialects. Indeed several of the words which have kept the pronunciation [ɑn] are found written *on* in medieval documents of certain parts of England. The same

---

[1] A list of the more important works on English Philology which have been consulted will be found in p. 12 of the chapter on "Language."

sound exists in some modern dialects: thus *branch* is pronounced [brɔntʃ] in Staffordshire. Now it is well known that
this *o*, in some Southern dialects, comes from an Old English
ā which becomes [*ǣ*] written *a* or *ai* in the North. French *an*,
having lost its nasal value in England, was assimilated to Old
English *a*, and followed the same evolution. As the change
a > o only began in the twelfth century, there seems to be no
reason why it should not have included the French *a*.

Thus the fate of French *a + n* has been the same as that of
Old English *a*: in English, *ă* remained unchanged, while *ā*
became *o* in certain parts of England from the twelfth century
onwards. Now, in English, a vowel followed by two consonants
was, generally speaking, short. As the same rule did not hold
good in French, there must have been much hesitation in the
pronunciation of French loan-words. This hesitation appears
in the spelling of [ɑn] which is, quite arbitrarily, it would seem,
either *an* or *aun*. For the same word in the same MS. is found
spelt either way, and moreover *an* rhymes with *aun*. The
spelling *aun*, where the *u*, as is frequently the case in English
manuscripts, served to show a long vowel[1], only lasted for a
comparatively short period, and scribes gave up *aun* entirely
in favour of *an*.

From this I draw the conclusion that the value of *a + n* was
settled as *short*, and that English loan-words in *on* are excep-
tions which date from the time when there was hesitation
between the long and the short *a*, or are purely dialectal.

The origin of the sound [ɔn] of such words as *haunt* can
easily be traced back to an English dialect. Thus we find in
a work certainly written and probably composed at Canterbury
in 1340, the *Ayenbite of Inwyt*, the following French words:
chonge, acquayntonce, penonce, marchons, etc. Now Canterbury
is in Kent, and the change *a > o* is one of the chief features of
the Kentish dialect.

ie.

Another Southern, and more especially Kentish, feature is
the use of *ie* for *e* or even *i*. Thus Gower writes *cliene* for *clene*.
This *ie* appears frequently in Anglo-Norman manuscripts and
has been generally attributed to Walloon influences. Without
going as far as to deny the possibility of such influences, I am
inclined to believe that the arguments in favour of an English
origin of Anglo-Norman *ie* are at least quite as strong.

---

[1] Cf. *oun*.

e > ae, ea.

The spelling *ae, ea* for *e* is common in Anglo-Norman manuscripts and is sometimes described as a *phonetic* feature. We might preferably see here the survival of the English spelling for *e*. In the South, *ae, ea* stand for an open *e*; in the North and the Midlands, the sound represented by *ae, ea* is an *a*. Thus there may be here an important test for settling the origin of certain works or manuscripts.

e mute.

The fall of *e* mute after the tonic vowel is a well-known feature of Middle English as well as Anglo-Norman phonetics. This accounts chiefly for the peculiar rhythm of French poetry in England.

A natural development of this phenomenon is the fall of the final *e* mute in Anglo-Norman not only as a prosodic value, but even in spelling. Thus we shall find the Infinitive *faire* spelt *fair*; thus too, a feminine ending can rhyme with a masculine.

In English likewise, the mute vowel can be elided or not, as I pointed out when discussing rhythm. We have instances of this as early as the twelfth century, e.g. in the *Moral Ode*, in purely English words. This phenomenon seems to appear in the North earlier than in the South and Midlands where the first instances occur in the fourteenth century.

This elision of the mute *e* has influenced the evolution of Anglo-Norman even more than that of Middle English: for it clearly explains the Anglo-Norman rhymes *é : ée*, and later the spelling *-ee* for a masculine *-é*. Lastly Infinitives in *-re* became *-er*, on the same principle as Middle English *bladdre* became *bladder*.

r and rr.

We cannot, as yet, draw definite conclusions as regards the use of the letter *r* in Anglo-Norman manuscripts. It is sometimes written *r*, sometimes *rr*, sometimes it is omitted altogether. It is clear, however, that the pronunciation of the *r*, in some parts of the country at least, must have been very weak: this consonant is often omitted at the end of a word in manuscripts, and thus many French Infinitives have the appearance of Participles.

This weakness of the *r* sound may therefore explain the vagaries of scribes in their use of *r* or *rr*. Few writers have been as careful in this respect as the author or scribe of the

Ormulum. He at least consistently marks short vowels by means of double consonants. I may, however, suggest, as an hypothesis worthy of further research, that, since the North alone has maintained in modern times a distinct pronunciation of the *r* sound, manuscripts where the *r* persists in all cases, where the double *r* is used regularly or does not occur, are probably documents originating from the North of England.

n or l "mouillés."

The so-called "consonnes mouillées" seem to have greatly puzzled our Anglo-Norman scribes. There is in fact frequent confusion between the ordinary *n* or *l* and the corresponding "mouillé" sound. To my mind, Continental influences have little to do with this confusion. We find in Walloon, for instance, four different spellings for the *n* "mouillé," all of which occur again in Anglo-Norman. But our scribes, in addition to those four spellings, offer us the choice between at least ten others. The conclusion is obvious: English writers of Anglo-Norman works had to render sounds difficult to reproduce and unknown in the English language. They expressed them as best they could, and each according to his own imagination, without any attempt at being consistent even in the course of the same manuscript. Hence, e.g., the following spellings for *n* "mouillé": *ni, ngn, gni, igni, ingi, ing, inc, ini, ign, in, inn, gn, ngi, ng, ni, nn, ignn, nni.*

s and z.

The confusion between *s* and *z*, so frequent in Anglo-Norman, is a well-known phenomenon in certain English dialects. Thus initial *z* for *s* is a distinctive feature of Kentish and of the modern Somerset dialect. The geographical boundaries of this change in Middle English are not yet settled. Intelligent co-operation between students of kindred subjects would doubtless help to solve the problem.

s and *z* final are particularly liable to confusion as, very early in the history of Anglo-Norman, *s* final had become mute. This will explain why we find here again a series of equivalents which are due far more to necessities of spelling than to phonetics.

English dialects are also doubtless the cause of other alterations in the French *s*. Thus I may mention the change of *s* + *l*, *n* to *d* + *l*, *n* (*isle* > idle, *mesler* > medler); the spellings *ht, ght*, etc. for *st* (*miht, conuht*, etc. in *Le Chevalier, la Dame et le Clerc*).

I now add briefly a few more Anglo-Norman forms which are probably due to English dialect influences, and I suggest, after each of them, their possible origin:

(*a*) Fall of *l* final (North?): *a* = *al*; *se* = *cel*, etc.

(*b*) *l* > *r* (found in most dialects): *nature*: *nule* (*Bestiaire*); *itel*: *mer* (*Apocalypse*).

(*c*) *n* + labial, or final > *m* (South?): *emfant, emfer, mum* (*Assomption*[1]).

(*d*) *n* > *gn* (North?): *peigne* (= English *pain*) (*Jugement Dernier*[2]).

(*e*) *r* falls before another consonant (South?): *sefs* (*Boeve*).

(*f*) *re* > *er* (South and West?): *ester, pernez* (*Boeve*).

(*g*) *r* inorganic (found in many dialects, more especially in the South): *ewangelistres*: *ministres* (*Jugement Dernier*).

(*h*) *t* final > *th* (North and West?)
    z final > *th* (North and West?)
oth (= *ot*) (*Psautier d'Arundel*).

I join here *th* < *t*, and *th* < *z*, for the change of *z* to *th* is not satisfactorily proved. It occurs in the 2nd person pl. where the ending -*ez* is spelt -*eth*. But the Anglo-Norman *th* rhymes in general with *t*: *toutes*: *couthes* (*Divisiones Mundi*). It is therefore very probable that Southern authors used the ending -*eth* instead of -*ez* without having any intention of representing one letter by another: for them -*eth* was the natural ending for the plural in the Southern Middle English conjugation, and they applied this ending to the Anglo-Norman verb. The plural ending in the North was -*es*, -*is*, or -*e*; in the Midlands -*en*, -*es*, or -*e*. Thus, just as we find the Southern ending -*eth* in some cases, we might expect to find -*en*, -*es*, -*is*, or -*e* in others: and indeed the ending -*e* for the 2nd person pl. occurs frequently in Anglo-Norman manuscripts. The importance of this remark is obvious and further study may allow us thereby to localize many of our Anglo-Norman manuscripts.

It must be admitted that, so far, few definite conclusions have been reached as regards the influence of English dialects on the formation of Anglo-Norman; but the subject is new, and there can be no progress until scholars co-operate and the mass of documents available has been closely studied and edited.

*   *   *

In the preceding pages I have merely endeavoured to lay foundations and to suggest a few salient points which are worthy of study; for we are still only on the fringe of a vast

---

[1] J. P. Strachey, *Poem on the Assumption*.
[2] H. J. Chaytor, *Poem on the Day of Judgment*.

subject. We have yet to recognize in Anglo-Norman the interesting outcome of a language introduced into a foreign country, forced by purely artificial means upon its inhabitants, and gradually yielding to the pressure of ethnological forces.

When this is admitted, the subject of Anglo-Norman becomes one of paramount interest to students of ethnology, history, art, literature and linguistics[1].

In conclusion, I must here thank Miss Strachey and Miss Halkett, whose very painstaking and careful phonetic studies of the *Poem on the Assumption* and of the *Divisiones Mundi* respectively have enabled me, with a minimum of labour to myself, to study the phonology of the three works which are printed in this volume.

*   *   *

The reader may now be able to appreciate our reasons for planning the edition of many texts which may have comparatively little literary value. The editors are at least unanimous on two points: the selection of material and the mode of editing. We have not always followed the methods adopted abroad in the case of Old French texts, for experience has taught us that certain conventions useful in the case of Continental texts could only be misleading when applied to Anglo-Norman.

Our editions are exact copies of the manuscripts. No corrections are introduced in the text; all suggested alternative readings or emendations are given in notes. Abbreviations are expanded and printed in italics, the form selected being in every case the one used most frequently by the author in cases where the syllable is written in full.

When two or more words have been run into one in a manuscript, they are divided, and the stops usual in modern texts have been introduced: this is a departure from our plan of strict adherence to the text of the author, but we thus convey to the reader our interpretation of many obscure passages.

The same remark applies to our use of accents, but here we diverge greatly from the Continental practice: we use neither the diaeresis nor the grave accent. Our Anglo-Norman scribes differed in their appreciation of the value of two consecutive vowels: some counted them as one syllable, some as two. A word may vary in the course of the same poem. Thus a

---

[1] The gist of this Preface formed the subject of an article which appeared in *Romania*, April–June, 1923.

diaeresis introduced strictly according to French etymology might be absolutely misleading.

As for the grave accent, it serves to distinguish an open from a closed *e*. Here again our poets are inconsistent, especially in later texts, when probably all phonetic difference between English and Anglo-Norman vowels had ceased to exist. It is, besides, an open question whether the distinction between open and close *e* has ever been more than academic, and many editors of Old French texts have their doubts as to the real difference between those sounds.

We therefore use only the acute accent on final *e* or *es when that e was pronounced open or close,* and on the feminine ending *-ée*.

The apostrophe is inserted whenever a vowel is elided before another vowel.

The cedilla is used to show a soft *c*.

I may add, in conclusion, that several of the remarks on phonetics which occur in the course of this Preface will be found again in the notes on our three texts: the reader will surely not blame me for making all references to points of philology as convenient as possible.

O. H. PRIOR

LANGUAGE

By O. H. Prior

(**A** = Poem on the Assumption. **B** = Day of Judgment. **C** = Divisiones Mundi.)

In the following pages we only deal with a few sounds which offer some interest by comparison between the three texts. Though we do not always draw conclusions from the forms or spellings quoted, students of Middle English dialects may find much useful and suggestive material in the following lists: *e.g. hout* for *haut* (**C** 671).

TONIC VOWELS

Ai

In **A** *ai* is written *ai* once only: *plaist* 15.
The usual spelling is *e*: *fet* 47 etc.
    ei is found as a protonic: *reisun* 41, *repeira* 121, etc.
In **B** *ai* is written *e*: *lesser* 3, *fet* 5, passim, *set* 14, *fet* 104.
    ai: *chair* 37.
    a: *faz* 57, *fas* 62.
    ei: *leiser* 58, *heire* 61, *veire* 62 (L. varium).
In neither **A** nor **B** do we find rhymes of *ai*: *e* or *ei*.
In **C** *ai* is written *ai*: *lais* 23, etc.
    ei: *estreit* 108, etc.
    e: *més* 24, etc.
    a: *a* 5 (L. habeo).
ai rhymes with *e*: *tere* : *repeire* 115, 6; 239, 40; 734, 5.
    fere : *tere* 177, 8.
    imés : *aprés* 842, 3.
There is therefore confusion in *spelling* in **A**, **B** and **C**. But only in **C** do we find a proof of the reduction of *ai* to *e*.

An

In **A** *a* + n is *never* written *aun*. This is one of our reasons for placing **A** before **B**: the spelling *aun* only appears towards the middle of the thirteenth century.

In **A** *an* does not rhyme with *en*; there is one laisse in *-an* (I), and one in *-en* (IX).

We find several spellings of *an* for *en*, but none of *en* for *an*: *sanz* 18 (< G. sinn); *sanz* 16 (< L. sine); *san* 96 (< L. sine).

In **B** we find both spellings, *an* and *aun* (*grant* : *taunt* 35, 36) but *aun* occurs only in the one case: *taunt* 36.

an does *not* rhyme with *en*.

a + n and *e* + n are carefully distinguished in spelling.

In **C** both spellings *an* and *aun* are used and are absolutely interchangeable, the same word being spelt indifferently with *an* or *aun*.

In the rhyme the scribe joins *an* and *aun*, or *an* and *an*, but never *aun* and *aun*.

Protonic *an* is never written *aun*.

A + n and *e* + n do not rhyme, and are kept distinct in spelling.

There is however one doubtful case: *tens* : *Adrians* 724, 725; but we hesitate about drawing conclusions from a rhyme connected with a proper name.

There are no rhymes therefore in our three poems which would tend to show a pronunciation other than that of an ordinary *a* before *n*, and we are inclined to think that the theory which saw in the spelling *aun* a mere sign of lengthening of the vowel (a theory which is generally accepted in the case of the parallel spelling *oun*) is after all the correct one. Even at a time when *aun* was freely used, in the fourteenth century, as in **C**, there is no method or consistency in the use of *aun*, and it does not seem to represent any sound distinct from *an*.

But there is the difficulty of explaining why French *an* appeared with two different pronunciations in English words of French origin, *i.e.* [an] as in *branch*, [ɔn] as in *haunt*.

We cannot help thinking that we have here the result of dialect influences. In Kent, in Middle English, [ɔn] seems to have been the regular pronunciation for [an]. The British Museum MS., Arundel 57, of the "Ayenbite of Inwyt," composed and written at Canterbury, *i.e.* Mid-Kent, in 1340, has the following spellings: acquaynt*o*nce, conten*o*nce, ch*o*nge, deliure*o*nce, pen*o*nce, march*o*ns, serg*o*nt, etc. All these are words of French origin which are now pronounced with [an] and not with [ɔn]. But it is reasonable to assume that other words were borrowed from the Kentish dialect and penetrated into the language with the Kentish [ɔn] pronunciation. According to this theory, the few words where *an* is pronounced [ɔn], *i.e.* haunt, avaunt, daunt, gaunt, jaunt, etc. would have entered the ordinary English language through the medium of the Kentish dialect. The great bulk of *an* words would have kept the more general pronunciation [an] but with a vowel, the quantity of which was doubtful: hence the hesitation of scribes who used sometimes *aun*, where *u* merely served to express length, sometimes *an*.

Ain

In **A** there are no rhymes in *ain* or *ein*. It is therefore impossible to say what was the value of those two sounds in this poem.

The spelling *ain* is usual, but in many cases *ain* is written *ein*: *einz* 29, *seinte* 61, *eime* 282, etc.

In **B** we find *ain* once only: *demain* 18.

Otherwise *ein*: *certeins* 39, *pleinte* 124, *sein* 19, etc.

There are no rhymes in *ain* or *ein*.

In **C** *ain* is written *ain* three times: 358, 423, 666.

ein three times: 233, 234, 316.

ain, written *ein*, rhymes with *ein*: *plein* : *certeinc* 315, 316.

Taprolainne (Taprobana): *plainne* (< L. plena) 289, 290, here *ein* is written *ain*.

loigtaines : *montagnes* 357, 358.

lointaine : *chene* (= chienne) 423, 424.

In **C** the rhymes seem to show great confusion. But it is probable that here, as in the case of *ai*, the pronunciation of *ai + n*, *ei + n* had become *e+n*. From that point of view, the last rhyme mentioned (*lointaine* : *chene*) is instructive. We can therefore assimilate the case of *ain*, *ein* to that of *ai* which was considered above. This was very likely, for all nasal vowels had lost their nasal value in Anglo-Norman, and further, final *n* or *m* were no longer pronounced. *N* or *m*, or even any one of the signs used for an "n mouillé," seem to be used indifferently as final spellings. This fact must be remembered when reading Anglo-Norman, as *ain*, *ein* frequently have the appearance of diphthongs ending in *i + n*.

Au

In **C** we note the spelling *ou* for *au* in "*hout*" = haut 671. This may be an instance of the change *a > o* which is a feature of English Midland and Southern dialects (*e.g.* O.E. āld > ōld).

Ié

In **A** *ié* : *é* : *lé* (< laetum) : *privé* 282, 283, etc.

ié is written *ie* or *e*.

In **B** *ié* (spelt *e*):*é*: *peché*: *purgé* 111, 112: *juger*:*mer* 101, 102, and several other Inf. where -*ier* > -*er*.

> *ié* spelt *e* occurs also in *cel* 86, 102; *ert* 111; *er* 125.
>
> *ié* spelt *ei* occurs in *ceil* 6 (the case is doubtful as the *e* is written above the *c* and it may stand for "ciel").

We may also quote here *veint* = vient 72.

ié spelt *i* occurs in *sicle* 55.

Except in *riens* 25, 105, the actual spelling *ie* does not occur, even before *n*.

In **C** the following cases prove nothing as to the rhyming of *ié*:*é*: *chet*:*siet* 738, 739; 870, 871; *chet*:*set* 103, 104; *sachez*:*peez* 553, 554.

There are only two cases of spelling with *ie* (739; 871).

The usual spelling is *e*.

There is only one example of the spelling *ee*: *peez* (554). This spelling *ee* for *ē* appears about 1250 in Middle English.

Old English *eo* generally gave *ē* in Middle English, except in Kentish where it gave *ie*. In French loan-words, *ie* likewise gave *e* in Middle English. We may therefore conclude that the sound or spelling *ie* may be accounted for, in Anglo-Norman as well as in Middle English, by the fact that the document is of Kentish origin.

Ei

In **A** *ei* does not rhyme with *e* (cf. laisses III and XIII in *ei*).

ei is written *ei*: *aveir* 11, etc.

> *e*: *saver* 18, *veer* 83.
> *i*: *aparilé* 159 (protonic).
> *ie*: *fie* 23 (vicem), *fiez* (vicem) 312.
> *oi*: *sumoila* 128 (protonic).

In **B** there are no rhymes *ei*:*e*.

ei is written *ei* or *oi*, which rhyme together: *averoit*: *gardereit* 41, 42; but there is a slight preponderance of *ei* forms.

In **C** *ei* rhymes once with *e* (=*ei*): *bevre*: *creire* 417, 418.

otherwise *ei*:*ei*, *e*:*e*.

ei is written *ei* in by far the greater number of cases.

ei is written *e* in seven cases.

ei is never written *oi*.

We have seen, when dealing with *ai*, that there were rhymes of *ai*:*ei*. It is noteworthy that *ei* is never written *ai*, and we may perhaps conclude that the pronunciation *ai* was rising to *ei*. Therefore if levelling of *ai*, *ei* took place in Anglo-Norman as it did in English, it must have been in the direction of *ei* rather than *ai*.

Both diphthongs are very early represented by *e*, though we cannot attach too much importance to that spelling in **A** as far as *ei* is concerned, since this *e* is only found in Infinitives.

As in the case of *ai*, we are inclined to think that the *e* represents a true stage of pronunciation, showing that both *ai* and *ei* were being monophthongized. The steps would be *ai > ei > e* (*i.e. é*, not *è*). As is well known this levelling of *ai, ei* and the subsequent monophthongization took place likewise in English[1]. But it is still a matter for discussion when and under what dialectal influence this change took place.

E

Our remarks are restricted to the treatment of post-tonic or protonic *e* and to the parasitic or svarabhaktic *e*.

In **A** *ée* rhymes with *é*: *gardée* 279, *honurée* 280 are found in a laisse in *é* (xi). In addition to that, there are several Past Participles after *être*, in this same laisse and in others, where *-ée* has been reduced to *-é*; though of course we may have to deal here with cases of non-agreement after the Participle. Still the two cases mentioned are sufficient proof of *ée : é*.

ée is written *e* in most cases where *ee* might be expected.

There are no clear cases of the fall of post-tonic *e* after a consonant. We find "*sumus*" 343.

Protonic e falls in many cases, *e.g. coiment* 231, *fra* 8, etc.

> becomes *i*: *espirit* 95, etc.
> becomes *a*: *rechaté* 343.
> becomes *u*: *sulun* 80.

Svarabhaktic e is found in *avereit* 98, etc.

In **B** there are no rhymes *ée : é*.

Post-tonic e after consonant falls in: *mund* 22, 101, *s'amend* 38. The spelling "*sumus*" 39 occurs also in **B**.

Protonic: *averoit* 41, etc.

In **C** *ée* rhymes with *é*: *cuntrées : pueplés* 343, 344, and many more cases.

ée is written *e*: *cuntré* 604, and many more.

Post-tonic e falls in: *mund* 185 (+ consonant), etc.

Consonant + e: consonant: *mere : deviser* 207, 208; *menvers : cheres* 513, 514. *pomes : devums* 473, 474, etc.

Protonic e is well maintained in **C**, whilst the forms of Future and Conditional: *savereit* 15, etc., are numerous.

[1] Cf. Wyld, *A Short History of English*, p. 152; Sweet, *History of English Sounds*, p. 186.

From the above remarks it appears that, in **A**, *e* falls more usually as a protonic than at the end of a word, except after *é*. **B** and **C** on the contrary maintain the protonic *e*. All three MSS. are consistent in their use of the svarabhaktic *e*.

There are instances of the fall of final *e* as early as the twelfth century in Middle English. It apparently took place earlier in the North than in the South and Midlands, where it only becomes regular in the fourteenth century[1]. The importance of this change for Anglo-Norman cannot be exaggerated; it is one of the factors, if not the chief factor, which explains 1° the use of -*e* for -*ée* (fem. end.), 2° the use of -*ee* for -*é* (m. end.), 3° the change or hesitation in the gender of many words, 4° the growth of the first conj. at the expense of the fourth (er < re[2]). A common and general practice in Middle English is the addition of an *e* before liquids or nasals, which may account for the widespread use of svarabhaktic *e* in Anglo-Norman.

Finally, an important criterion for the localisation of Anglo-Norman works might be found in the fact, noted by Morsbach, that, of two *e*'s in a polysyllable, preferably the last *e* is suppressed very early in the *North*, the *first e* disappears rather later in the *South*.

O free

In **A**, *O* free is written *u* : *tut* 30, *valur* 55, *hure* 180, *puple* 251, etc.

    eu : *deus* (duos) 229.

    oo : *voot* (voluit) 195, *vot* (voluit) 190 passim.

    ue : *quers* 66.

    uo : *quor* 80 passim.

There are no rhymes in *o*; one laisse (VI) is in *o* + *n*, which is consistently spelt *un*.

In **B**, *O* free is written *o* : *pople* 96, *jor* 116, *ore* 36, 71.

    u : *nus* (nos) 23, *joius* 24, *hure* 14, *devure* 13, *jur* 16, *fu* (=feu) 87, etc.

    ou : *jour* 75, 76.

    eu : *eure* (horam) 66.

In **C**, *O* free is written *o* : *mot* 88, etc., *enclot* 87 ⎫

    ou : *devourent* 483 ⎪

    e : *ef* 61, *evre* 1, *deskevre* 2 ⎬ *ǒ*

    eu : *preuf* 62 ⎭

    u : *tuz* 74, *dute* 91, etc. ⎫ *ō*

    ou : *chalour* 153, *boute* 508, etc. ⎭

---

[1] Cf. Luick, *Historische Grammatik der Englischen Sprache*, p. 540.

[2] Cf. bladdre > bladder (Luick, *o.c.* p. 544).

Rhymes: $o:ou:e:eu:ef$: *preuf* 61, 62.

$u:ou:o:e.$

$\bar{u}:\breve{o}$: *pus* (= plus) : *truis* 181, 182.

$\bar{u}:\bar{o}$: *desuz* (= super) : *tuz* 73, 74.

An interesting spelling is that of *ef* 61, *evre* 1. We seem to have here an instance of the Middle English change of [ǿ] to *e*, a change which took place in the thirteenth century[1]. If, as Wyld suggests, the change from Old English *eo* to *e* did not pass through the [ϕ] stage in the North, the East Midlands, and the South-East, we have here an additional argument in favour of a Western origin of **C** (for we find here the rhyme *ef*: *preuf* 61, 62), and perhaps also of **A** and **B**, where we have the spelling *eu* in one or two cases. We do not, however, lay much stress on these last spellings which are far more likely to be French in origin.

Perplexing rhymes are those of *pus* : *truis*, *desuz* : *tuz* in **C**, for we may have here instances of an important criterion for the localisation of texts. The rhyme $o:u$ [y] is notably a characteristic of Northern MSS. in Middle English, and the same feature, as Suchier has shown, is found in Anglo-Norman works hailing from the North. What are we to think of the presence of such a rhyme in a work which many other arguments, literary, historical and linguistic, oblige us to classify among South-Western documents? There is no doubt that *desuz* stands for *dessus* and not *dessous*; the Latin original has "*superius* coelum," and the spelling *uz* undoubtedly stands for [y] as well as for [u] + z (cf. *cruz* 415). We can only suggest, either that $u:o$ extended further South-West about the fourteenth century, or that $u>[\bar{u}]$, and thus we should have a normal rhyme in [ū] (cf. also Wyld's suggestion as to the spreading of the change $\bar{o}$ to [ū] in the South-West, *o.c.* pp. 106, 107).

CONSONANTS

H

H is prefixed in *hunt* (= ont) in **B** 36,
in *hausi* (= aussi) in **C** 654.

K

K is written *ch* in **C**: *Aufrike* : *afich* 189, 190, etc.; perhaps also *sach* 61 in **B**. In Middle English the spelling *ch* for *k* is always used at the initial in Domesday Book. It is noteworthy that, as early as the twelfth century, this use of *ch* is current in the South.

---

[1] Cf. Wyld, *o.c.* p. 109.

M and N

In **A** *m* final is spelt *n* in *nun* 51 (nomen).

n final is spelt *m* in *mum* 278, etc.

n final falls in *su* (suum) 51.

n is written *m* in *emfer* 344.

n is written *l* in *alme* 196.

n falls in *eprist* 183.

n mouillé written *n*: *guainer* 12.

mm: *humme* 7, *femme* 129, *communement* 254.

nn: *annuncia* 264.

In **B** *m* final in *venim* 26, in 1st pers. pl. *morum* 39, etc.

mm : *summe* (: *home* 7, 8), *comme* 108 (but *coment* 107, passim).

n is written *l* in *alme* 32.

n is written *gn* (*i.e.* n mouillé) in *peigne* 76.

m : *n* : *abime* : *vermine* 31, 32.

In **C** *m* final is spelt *n* in *nun* (nomen) 678, 771.

n final is spelt *m* in 1st pers. pl. *fesum* 40, etc.

n is written *m* in *emfauntent* 442.

n falls in *efante* 431.

mm, *nn* are frequent.

m : *n* : *resun* : *fesum* 39, 40.

n : *m* : *nn* : *mm* : *n* mouillé : *moienne* : *logtaine* 665, 666, etc.

                sone : *Escaloigne* 686, 687, etc.

                montagnes : *loigtaines* 357, 358, etc.

It is clear that in the rhyme there is no difference between *n* and *m*, and that *n mouillé* is assimilated to *n*, *m*.

Moreover, the *u* rhyme, *chescuns* : *ceus* 453, 454 **C**, shows that the *n* was not pronounced, at least before a consonant.

The following facts, which seem to be sufficiently established as far as Middle English is concerned, might well be studied in connection with Anglo-Norman *m* and *n*:

1. The loss of final *n* began in the *North* in the Old English period and extended *southwards* in the Middle English period. But *n* was only lost when it was strictly final (before a pause) or when it occurred before a consonant[1].

2. *m* + t, p > *n* in the West in Middle English.

3. *n* final becomes *m* in a weak final syllable of some dissyllabics stressed on the first syllable[2].

---

[1] Cf. O. Jespersen, *A Modern English Grammar*, I, p. 31.

[2] Cf. O. Jespersen, *o.c.* p. 29.

R

In **A** *r* falls before a consonant : *domant* 2.

    rr for *r* : *serra* 37, passim, etc.

    r for *rr* : *tere* 69, passim, etc.

    r inorganic after *st* : *estré* 58.

    r final : in laisse VII (in *-er*) *munter* is spelt *munte*.

In **B** *r* is never doubled, even when *rr* might reasonably be expected : cf. *tere* 102.

    r final : omitted in *flestri* = flestrir 57.

In **C** *r* falls before a consonant: *vedur* 314.

    rr for *r* : *serra* 31, etc.

    r for *rr* : *tere* 260, etc.

    r inorganic, after *st* : *ewangelistres* : *ministres* 812, 813.

    r : *rr* : *enserre* : *tere* 259, 260.

    metathesis of *r* : *pernent* 306, 307.

    r final : omitted in *mustré* 341, *froisé* (= froiser) 581.

The complete absence of *rr* in **B** is a striking fact for which we cannot venture to offer an explanation : the treatment of *r* in Middle English has not yet been sufficiently studied for conclusions to be drawn. The weak pronunciation of final *r* is proved by the Infinitives in which this *r* has been dropped in **A**, **B** and **C**. Metathesis of *r*, especially + *n* or *s*, is frequent in the West and South, and was already common in Old English. The uniform treatment of *r* in **B** may be the result of a strong pronunciation of this consonant, which, if we are to judge by Modern English standards, would be distinctive of the *North*.

S

In **A** *ss* : *messe* 73, etc.

    s for *ss* : *asez* 275, etc.

    s + consonant falls in *meme* 180.

    s final falls : *for* (L. foris) 213, *san* (L. sine) 96.

    s final written *z* : *jurz* 269, *sanz* 16, etc.

In **B** *ss* : *lesser* 3, etc.

    c for *ss* : *enbracer* 4, etc.

    s for *ss* : *richese* 63, etc.

    sc for *ss* : *tristesce* 36.

    s + consonant falls : *abime* 31.

    s final written *z* : *voz* 45, etc.

    s final written *s* : *vus* 28, etc.

    s final silent : *plurs* : *dolur* 75, 76.

    s : *ss* : *richese* : *hautesse* 63, 64, etc.

    s never rhymes with *z*.

In **C** *ss*: *amasse* 59, etc.

s for *ss*: *asez* 169, etc.

sc for *ss*: *veillesce* 403, etc.

s final written *s*: *ceus* 453, etc.

s final written *c*: *certeinc* 316.

s written *c*: *deck* 12.

ss : *ss*: *amasse* : *grasse* 59, 60.

s + *l* becomes *d* + *l*: *idle* 288.

The change *s* + *l* to *d* + *l* alone requires a note. This change is well-established by such English words as "medlar," etc. *sl* could not give *dl* directly, nor could *dl* be the result of a *d* inserted as a glide sound between *s* and *l*. It is more likely that *s* became first of all *z* according to the Old English rule that *s* between two voiced sounds became voiced, except when *s* was doubled. Thus the stages here would be sl > [zl] > dl[1].

T and D.

In **A** *t* final becomes *d*: *ad* 40, *parlad* 243.

t final falls: *secre* 67, *servi* 50, etc.

d final becomes *c*: *defenc* (L. defendo) 253.

d falls: *responeit* 331.

In **B** *t* final is omitted in *er* 125.

t final remains: *serat* 10, *vat* 66.

t final becomes *d*: *ad* 9, passim.

t : *d*: *ad* : *serat* 9, 10; *ad* : *vat* 65, 66; *ensement* : *s'amend* 37, 38.

In **C** *t* final remains: *vet* 478, etc.

t final becomes *d*: *ad* 258, etc.

t : *d*: *mund* : *sunt* 3, 4, passim.

t : *th*: *tretutes* : *cothes* 361, 362.

The treatment of final *d* or *t* is especially noteworthy in verbal endings, and here more clearly than anywhere else we are able to trace the direct influence of dialects.

In Middle English the pres. ind. is treated as follows[2]:

South and Kent		East Midlands		West Midlands		North	
Sing.	Pl.	Sing.	Pl.	Sing.	Pl.	Sing.	Pl.
1 -e		-e		-e		-e	
2 -est	-eþ	-est	-en, -es, -e	-es, -est	-es, -en, -us, -un	-es	-es, -is, -e
3 -eþ		-eþ, -es		-es		-es	

[1] Cf. Wyld, *o.c.* p. 67; Jespersen, *o.c.* p. 47.   [2] Mostly after Wyld, *o.c.* p. 193.

In the South the *e* in the endings -est, etc. is frequently syncopated. To these remarks we must add that in early Southern Middle English final *d* is unvoiced and is written *t*, while in later Southern Middle English the *d* is restored[1].

We can see therefore that the tendency was, to keep the final consonant in verbs, but that there was, in the South at least, much hesitation in the use of *d* and *t*. Our documents confirm these two facts: the 3rd sing. generally ends in a consonant, and t:d. We have already noticed the tendency to omit the final *e* in Middle English: hence numerous forms such as *amend* (cf. *os* = ose:*monoceros*, C 541, 542). A most important test of dialect is found in the 2nd pl. *-eþ* in the South, *-es*, *-en* or *-e* in the Midlands (for the *-e* forms, cf. Morsbach[2]), *-es*, *-is*, *-e* in the North.

The *-eþ* has been retained in C, where it is written *-eth* (106, 586, 834, 858) or *-et* (109, 700, 875). We saw above that *th* rhymed with *t* (*tretutes* : *cothes*). Several 2nd pers. pl. which end in *t* (71, 109, etc.) would prove that for our author or scribe the 2nd pl. really ended in *-eþ* as in Middle English and not in *-ez*, as in French. The spelling *-ez* is found however (*oiez* 584, etc.) and even *-es* (*volés* : *lez* 589, 590). This means that in Anglo-Norman the verbal endings of both French and English could be used side by side. This survival of Middle English verbal inflections explains why the 2nd pers. pl. ending can frequently be found spelt *-e*: it points to a Midland or Northern document or writer, but the South is excluded.

Thus *este* 27 in B places our MS. in the Midlands or North.

voleth 106 in C places our MS. in the South.

Another South Irish document which we hope to publish later contains the same feature (*-eth* in 2nd pl.) and confirms our opinion that South Western English was spoken in the South of Ireland in the thirteenth century.

A contains no abnormal forms in the 2nd pl. and must therefore be placed according to other tests.

W

In A *w* does not occur.

In B *w* = *v*: *ewe* 102.

In C *w* = *v*: *ewe* 114, etc.

  = *u*: *cowe* 503, passim.

  = *vu*: *awm* 651, passim.

---

[1] Cf. Sweet, *o.c.* p. 198.   [2] Morsbach, *Mittelenglische Grammatik*, p. 106.

Z

In **C** alone can $s:z$. Also $s = z$ in the interior of the verse. There is therefore confusion between the voiced and voiceless consonant in **C**, but not in **A** and **B**.

The Middle English practice as regards *s* and *z* is thus stated by Sweet[1]: *þ, s, f* were voiced *everywhere* (*i.e.* in any position) in the South and Kent, except in such combinations as *st*.

Wyld[2], discussing Old English consonants, says: "*s* and *f* were pronounced as voiceless consonants when final; initially in the West Saxon dialect, they were apparently voiced before vowels; medially between vowels, they were always voiced."

The same dialectal differences would no doubt explain the English words of French origin: confessor, message, possible, etc. with [s] voiceless in both French and English, but: possession, dissolve, design, resemble, etc. with [z] voiced in English, but the voiceless [s] in French.

This whole question is, however, still a matter for discussion.

* * *

Necessities of space prevent us from dealing with further points; for the same reason questions of morphology are not being dealt with in this volume. Still, in the small space allotted, we have tried to break new ground, being convinced that Anglo-Norman phonology is to a great extent based on the Middle English of the period, and perhaps even forestalls Middle English documents in the correct rendering of the evolution of sounds.

As certain parts of England, the North in particular, are scantily represented in Middle English literature, much information might be derived from properly located Anglo-Norman documents.

A parallel study of Middle English and Anglo-Norman must necessarily produce fruitful results in both languages.

REFERENCES

D. Behrens, *Französische Elemente im Englischen* in Paul's *Grundriss der Germanischen Philologie*, Band I, pp. 950–989.

A. J. Ellis, *On Early English Pronunciation.* (5 vols., 1867–1889.)

O. Jespersen, *A Modern English Grammar*, 2 vols. (Heidelberg, 1909.)

M. Kaluza, *Historische Grammatik der Englischen Sprache.* (2 vols., Berlin, 1900.)

K. Luick, *Historische Grammatik der Englischen Sprache.* (Leipzig, 1914, etc.) We have only been able to make use of the first six parts of this most valuable work; fortunately the last two parts cover a large part of our ground.

R. Morris, *Historical Outlines of English Accidence.* (London, Macmillan, 1897.)

L. Morsbach, *Mittelenglische Grammatik.* (Halle, 1896.)

H. Sweet, *History of English Sounds.* (Oxford, 1888.)

F. J. Tanquerey, *L'évolution du verbe en anglo-français.* (Paris, 1915.)

J. Wright, *The English Dialect Grammar.* (Oxford, 1905.)

H. C. Wyld, *A Short History of English.* (London, Murray, 1914.)

---

[1] Sweet, *o.c.* p. 191.   [2] Wyld, *o.c.* p. 67.

POEM ON THE ASSUMPTION

EDITED BY J. P. STRACHEY

INTRODUCTION

1. Manuscript. The MS. in which the poem is preserved belongs to Pembroke College, Cambridge. It is thus described by Dr M. R. James:
"No. 112. Excerpta de moralibus Gregorii etc.
Vellum, 7 × 5¾, ff. 96, a good many tracts bound together. Cent. xii, xiii, in many good hands....Perhaps from Bury, but not entered by James or Wren: possibly therefore from Reading." (*A Descriptive Catalogue of the Manuscripts in the Library of Pembroke College, Cambridge*, p. 108.)
The Anglo-Norman poem is the last in the volume, ff. 93–96. It is written as though in prose.

2. Source. The source of the poem is Chapters 31 and 32 of Book II of the Visions of St Elizabeth of Schönau. St Elizabeth, like her contemporary St Hildegard, was a nun who became famous for her visions, in which she conversed with Christ, the Virgin and the Saints, and received instruction in matters of faith. She was born in 1129, and probably belonged to a noble family of the Middle Rhenish district. In 1141, at the age of twelve, she came to the convent of Schönau, which was attached to the Benedictine monastery of the same name. Schönau was situated on the mountain of Lichtborn, in Nassau, and had been founded in 1124 or 1125 by Count Rupert of Lurenburg. The first Abbot was Hildelin; the nuns were under the supervision of the monastery, and were ruled by a Prior and a Mistress. Elizabeth probably took the veil in 1147, at the age of eighteen; the visions began in 1152, when she was twenty-three. She was made Mistress of the convent in about 1157, and died on June 18th, 1164.

It seems probable that in the first instance the visions were noted down by Elizabeth and some of her nuns, partly in Latin and partly in German, but they were then re-written in a more elegant Latin by Elizabeth's brother, Egbert, a monk who came to Schönau in about 1155, and succeeded Hildelin as Abbot in 1165 or 1166.

Besides three Books of Visions, St Elizabeth also wrote the Liber Viarum Dei (probably modelled on St Hildegard's Scivias), an account of St Ursula and the Eleven Thousand Virgins of Cologne, and a certain number of letters to different abbots, abbesses, monks and nuns. Her works were widely known in the Middle Ages, and are contained in many MSS. in Germany, France and England. The most complete of these is that which was copied at Schönau at the end of the twelfth century, and is now in the Landesbibliothek at Wiesbaden. This contains, besides the works mentioned above, a Prologue by Egbert, and a short account of the Saint's life, giving the date at which the visions began, the circumstances in which they occurred, and the manner in which they were, for the most part, written down from the Saint's own narrative[1].

The version on which the Anglo-Norman poem is based belongs to a group of MSS. which contain only the Vision of the Assumption (chapters 31 and 32 of Book II), preceded by the two first sentences of the life. Two such MSS. are at Oxford (Bodl. Laud. Misc. 359, Lincoln xxviii).

On the whole the Anglo-Norman poem follows the Latin text fairly closely. Lines 51–71 render the facts contained in the two introductory sentences, and the poet then goes on to the account of the Vision of the Assumption. The following differences may be noted:

(*a*) the Latin narrative is told in the first person; the A.N. poem speaks of the Saint always in the third person.

(*b*) in the A.N. poem the Saint is called 'Ysabel' throughout.

(*c*) the A.N. poem does not give the name of the convent to which St Elizabeth belonged, though it is mentioned as being in the diocese of Treves.

(*d*) in the Latin version the vision of the Assumption is stated to have taken place 'in anno quod michi per angelum domini annuntiabatur liber viarum dei,' *i.e.* A.D. 1156, the fifteenth year after Elizabeth became a nun. In the A.N. poem the Vision is referred to the eleventh year (ll. 60 and 70–71). Here the poet is clearly following the introduction, where the eleventh year is spoken of as that in which the visions in general began.

3. **Subject.** The subject of the poem is the question of the bodily Assumption of the Virgin. This had been long debated, but the truth was finally revealed to Ysabel (St Elizabeth), in a series of visions of the Virgin. On the first occasion (August 23, 1156), Ysabel

---

[1] Cf. *Die Visionen und Briefe der hl. Elisabeth, nach den Original-Handschriften herausgegeben von F. W. E. Roth* (2nd ed. Brünn, 1886). The information contained in this work as to the Latin MSS. in England needs completing and correcting.

asks what has become of the Virgin's body, but is told that the time is not yet come for the truth to be made known. A year later (August 15, 1157), Ysabel sees the complete vision of the Assumption, and the meaning of what she has seen is explained to her by her familiar angel. A week later (August 22), the angel returns, and tells her that the date at which the Assumption took place was the fortieth day after the Virgin's death. Two years later (August 15, 1159) the Virgin appears and gives Ysabel leave to relate privately what she has seen. At the Virgin's next appearance, Ysabel is informed that she lived for a year after the death of Christ, and that the apostles were all summoned to her death bed. On March 25, the Feast of the Annunciation, the Virgin again appears, and tells Ysabel that she was fifteen years old at the Annunciation.

4. Other versions in French literature. Another version of St Elizabeth's Vision of the Assumption in French verse exists in Paris, at the Bibliothèque Nationale (MS. 818). It is quite independent of the Anglo-Norman poem, and professes to be a direct translation:

> D'Elisabet l'ancelle dé
> Voil metre ce q̄ nai trové
> dedenz son livre en escrit....

DE LE ASSUMPTIUN NOSTRE DAME KE FU REVELÉE A UNE NONEIN

I

Recto 1 f. 93

1 Parfunde questiun e grant
ne puet nus hom soldre en domant[1]:
viste sen demande e vaillant
oscure chose enquerant.
5 Més la chose puet neparquant[2]
tant estre oscure, e tant fuiant
sen de humme, e itant suzpernant,
rien n'i fra, si deu avant
n'i mette sa grace e sun grant
10 d'entendre iço k'il va chaçant[3]:

---

[1] *domant:* (?) corr. dormant. Cf. Preface, p. xxiv, Remarks on *r.* [2] *neparquant:* the scribe has used the contraction which usually stands for *par, per* (cf. also l. 192). [3] ll. 1–10, *Trans.:* A deep and great question no man can solve in sleep: to examine an obscure thing requires a quick and solid mind. But yet the thing may be so obscure, and so transcending the mind of man, and so surprising, that nothing will avail if God do not put forward his grace and his desire, and give understanding of what the mind is pursuing.

tel quide aveir vet esluignant,
e tel guainer ki va perdant.
Més deus est pius e tant suffrant,
tant duz, tant bons, e tant vailant,
15 bien li plaist sa grace uverant,
sanz ki nuls n'est de rien poant.
Kar ço ke humme, tant seit sachant,
ne puer[1] saver, (kar sanz failant
li va quant en sei desturnant)
20 Deu par sa grace va mustrant,
e de poi sage fait savant.
Suvent par miracle fesant,
acune fie en revelant
par sei, u par les suens mandant,
25 a suens dunt ainz furent dutant
par sa grace vet acertant,
e pus par eus revient avant
a ces k'iço vunt demandant;
e ço dunt einz furent dutant
30 devient tut cler al oil parant[2].

II

Bien de lung tens est duté,
de la dame dunt deu fu né
si sen cors est resuscité
u nun, e a glorie mené;
35 u uncore seit en terre estué,
e deske al jugement gardé,
u bon e mal serra jugé,
e aprés seit glorifié,
e plus ke autre en bien fermé.
40 Més deus de quant ke il ad crié
seit la reisun, tens ad granté
e liu a quant k'il ad furmé[3],

---

[1] *puer*: corr. *puet*.   [2] ll. 17–30, *Trans.*: For that which a man, however full of knowledge he may be, cannot know (for his mind fails him when it turns to and fro on itself), God shows by his grace, and makes the simple learned. Often by performing a miracle, sometimes by his own revelation, or by imparting it to his chosen, he shows to his chosen by his grace the truth of that of which they doubted, and then through them it is shown to those who enquire about it; and that which formerly they doubted becomes clear to the eye and evident. [3] MS. fĕrme.

dunt seit quant deit estre mustré[1].
De dutance nus ad jeté,
45 mustré nus ad la verité
de ço dunt ai la sus parlé,
questiun fet, e travailé,
par une dame ke a gré
la dame dunt deus fu encharné
50 servi mut a volenté[2].
Su nun fu Ysabel numé,
ke de Trevres en la vesché
a une abbeie[3] ad demuré
ake de tens, u tant munté

Verso 1 f. 93 b

55 est en valur e en seinté
ke aparcevent est revelé
a lui ço ke tant est celé
a tut ki avant unt estré[4];
unke tant ne fu acuinté.
60 Le unzime[5] an esteit ja entré
ke en seinte vie ot cunversé,
el tens Hiltus[6], une bone abbé,
ke lui e mut autres ot gardé,
nimeins, e bien endoctriné,
65 deu criendre e amer enseigné,
kant ses quers de deu espiré
vit le cunseil e le secré
del cors sa mere, s'est levé
al ciel u en tere lessé.

III

70 L'unzime ja venu esteit
ke Ysabel rendu se aveit,
e al utime jur tut dreit,
a la messe cum ele seeit,
ke l'en de feste feseit
75 del assumptiun, ne creeit

---

[1] ll. 40–43, *Trans.:* But God knows the reason of whatever he has created, and has given time and place to whatever he has formed, by which he knows when it shall be shown. [2] ll. 48–50, *Trans.:* a lady who constantly according to her will and pleasure served the lady in whom God was incarnated. [3] The abbey of Schönau. [4] *estré:* corr. *esté.* [5] *unzime:* in reality the vision of the Assumption took place in the fifteenth year after St Elizabeth became a nun: cf. Introduction. [6] *Hiltus:* the Latin form is Hildelinus, which should give *Hillins* in French.

pas nul ke ço ne savereit
de quele joie sis quers ardeit.
A rien s'a deu nu*n* n'entendeit;
tut ublié le mund aveit
80 sun q*u*or; sulu*n* ço ke veeit,
s'en de la remuer teneit,
qu*a*nt la dame q*u'e*le soleit
suvent veer, a lui veneit,
e aparut, e bien saveit
85 k'ele fu, ainz li feseit
suvent solaz e cunforteit
tutes ures k'ele vuleit.
E mest*er* fust pas, ne n'aveit,
se ubliée ore sereit[1].
90 La dame vint e li diseit:
—d'un frere[2] loé li esteit—
"Duce dame, se v*us* ple'seit,
mu*n* q*u*or de v*us* mut desireit[3]
saveir sentir ke creire deit[4]:
95 si li vostre espirit sereit,
san le cors ke tant e*st* beneit,
glorifié? Ke ço savereit,
dutance g*r*ant osté avereit;
apr*és* dut*er* nus ne p*ur*reit,
100 ne nul mes de ço ne mescrereit."

IV

Atant la dame dit li a:
"Ço ke tu quers pas ne serra
mustré p*ar* tei; nel savera
nuls ore, més tens puis vend*r*a,
105 e tost, gueres ne demurra,
ke deus p*ar* tei le mustera[5],

---

[1] ll. 80–89, *Trans.*: according to what she saw she refrained on that account from moving in that place, when the lady whom she was accustomed to see often came to her and appeared, and she (Ysabel) knew well who she was, for she often gave her solace and comfort whenever she wished, and there would have been no need, nor was there, that she should be forgotten now.   [2] *un frere*: cf. the Latin: "sicut ab uno ex senioribus nostris premonita fueram," cf. also l. 115.   [3] *desireit*: 3 sg. conditional: cf. below l. 326, and Tanquerey, *Evol. du Verbe*, p. 704.   [4] ll. 92–94, *Trans.*: Sweet lady, if it pleased you, my heart would much wish to be able to hear what it ought to believe.   [5] *mustera*: 3 sg. future of *mustrer*: cf. Tanquerey, p. 708.

ço que de mei atanz cela.”

Ysabel, quant ço oit a,

trestut cel an se reposa

110   d'enquere ço que demanda

de la dame; pas n'en osa,

ne lui ne l'angle a ki parla,

ki a lui suvent se mustra,

e privé fu, e cunforta.

115   Més un frere ki la garda

un ureisun li comanda

chescun jur dire de si la,

que par lui ço que desira

fust mustré. Poi puis demura

120   ke li ans fu acompli ja,

e la grant feste repeira

de la dame, que l'em numa

le assumptiun, dunt em chanta

la messe. Ysabel regarda

125   e de luin vit, ço li sembla,

un sepulcre u avisa

lumere grant que aviruna

le sepucre u sumoila

un cors que femme figura.

V

130   A cel cors mut ad regardé;

bien fu sun quor en haut levé,

e sur sei ravi e munté[1].

Quant teu cho chose[2] li est mustré,

tut le siecle entreublié.

135   Mut ja a ço uveré

li grant maus que ele ot encuntré,

dunt sen cors tant fu travailé

lung tens devant[3]; fu bien purgé

de peché par l'enfermeté

140   quant par grace li fu duné

veie[4] que tant ad desiré.

---

[1] Cf. the Latin: "veni in mentis excessum cum labore vehementi."   [2] *teu cho chose* : corr. *teu chose.*   [3] Cf. the Latin : "languebam egritudine dierum multorum."   [4] *veie* : in the MS. v̈ẽe.

Entur le cors mut grant clarté
des angles vit, qui l'unt levé
sus de terre e porté;
145 a munt au ciel l'unt cunveé,
e al porter adés chanté.
Atant le cors ad encuntré
uns hoem mut beaus od grant clarté.
Iteus n'est nuls home né;
150 ne tut cil que sunt encharné
puis ke li mund fu estoré,
se trestuz fusent asemblé,
ne puissent sa glorie e sa beauté
mustrer. Le fiz deu
155 sur rien resembler[1] ad e porté
ad une croiz[2] u fu fermé
une enseigne, e ferm lacé;
od lui angles a grant plenté
vindrent tut aparilé,
160 de lui servir bien asmé,
mil mielers de angles enumbré[3];
e a grant chant la sus mené
od sun fiz en ciel alé.

VI

Aprés iço si petit nun   Verso 2 f. 94 b
165 demura puis la visiun.
La dame ki redemptiun
a tuz dune, e remissiun
de noz pechez par le barun
que ele cunçut, ke aveit nun
170 Jesus, ki la maleiçun
esteinst e duna beneiçun
a tuz iceus ki sun sermun
e sa parole e sa raisun
crerunt en revelatiun,
175 se mustra. Grant refectiun

---

[1] Corr. *resemblé*.   [2] *Corr.*: le fiz deu resemblé | ad sur rien, e ad porté | une croiz. Cf. the Latin: "vir supra omnem estimationem gloriosus, portans in dextera signum crucis, in quo et vexillum apparuit, quem intelligebam esse ipsum dominum salvatorem."   [3] Enumbré: the French *ennombrer* means "to number"; here it seems to mean "innumerable." Cf. the Latin: "infinita milia angelorum."

de joie lui fu a fuisun
q*u*ant sa glorificatiun
a lui mus*tra*; tel mustreisun
ne fu sanz g*r*ant dilectiun.

VII

180 En meme le hure vit ester
un angle a ki soleit p*ar*ler
devant suvent, e dema*n*der
ep*ri*st meintena*n*t signifier
q*ue* ço deveit q*ue* vit port*er*
185 angles cel cors, le ciel mu*n*ter[1].
E il li dist: "P*ur* tei mustrer
ço dunt soleies q*ue*reler
del cors, de la char dut*er*,
de lui dunt deu voot encharner.
190 Deu te vot p*ar* ço ac*er*ter,
q*ue* as ci veu, q*u'*a sest munté,
en car, en os le ciel p*ar*cer
la fist[2], e puis resuscit*er*.
Plenierem*en*t glorifier
195 la voot, q*u*ant od lui aluer,
e cors e alme au ciel men*er*[3]."
E puis ap*ré*s al rep*ar*irer
del setime jur, revisit*er*
li angle vint. De lui pr*e*er
200 ne ublia pas q*ue* enseign*er*
li vosistist[4], dire e acuingt*er*,
q*u*ant deu la vot resusciter,
e certeinme*n*t le jur numer.
E il dist: "Bien le deit[5] grant*er*;
205 unkes p*ur* el cha enveer
ne vot[6] la dame, q*u'*a am*er*

---

[1] ll. 180–185, *Trans.:* At the same hour she saw standing an angel to whom before she had often been accustomed to speak, and she began at once to ask what this should mean, that she saw angels carry this body and go up to heaven.
[2] ll. 191–193, *Corr.:* qu'a sest munter, | en car, en os le ciel porter | la fist.
[3] ll. 190–196, *Trans.:* God wishes to assure you by what you have seen here, that by this raising he had her carried up to heaven in flesh and bone, and then resuscitated. He wished to glorify her fully, to place her with him, and to lead her to heaven both in body and soul.   [4] *vosistist:* corr. *vosist.*   [5] *deit: i.e.* the Virgin.   [6] *ne vot:* corr. *me vot* (?).

avez enprise, e anurer,
pur deu sur tut en tuz loer[1].

VIII

La verité saveir volez.
210 Dirai la vus; ore l'entendez:
de la feste que est apelez
le assumptium ne sunt passez
for vint e vint jurz[2] esculez,
que li cors fu resuscitez
215 de la dame, el ciel levez
u od suen fiz est aluez
e hautement glorifiez.
Et pur ço ke nuls acertez
fu de suen cors, se fust muntez
220 au ciel u nun, si fu numez
sa feste, que est celebrez
devant septembre e honurez[3],
dormitiun, e puis asez
l'assumptiun dit, e gardez
225 en joie, a grant solempnitez:
ki bien crerunt[4], bien le creez,
que en terre ne fust muscez
le cors de lui dunt deu fu nez[5]."

IX

Deus ans aprés entierement   Recto 3 f. 95
230 puis la visiun, humblement
Ysabel se tint, e coiment.
Rien ne parla, sacez n'i ment,

---

[1] ll. 205–208, *Trans.:* for no other reason does the lady wish to send me here, whom you have undertaken to love and honour, and for God's sake to praise above and in all things.   [2] Forty days from August 15th = September 23rd, which was kept by some of the Bavarian dioceses, and those of Brandenburg, Mainz, Frankfurt, etc., as the feast of the "Second Assumption."   [3] *i.e.* August 15th.
[4] *crerunt:* possibly an example of an A.N. 3 pl. preterite ending in *-unt:* the sense requires a past (cf. the Latin "quia etiam carne assumptam indubitanter credebant," and Tanquerey, p. 244).   [5] ll. 218–228, *Trans.:* and because no one knew for certain as to her body, if it had gone up to heaven or not, her feast which is celebrated and honoured before September was called Dormition, and then some time after was called the Assumption, and was kept with joy and great solemnity; for indeed they believed, believe it well, that the body of her of whom God was born was not hidden in the earth.

kar mut duta la male gent,
s'en eust parlé, contrevement
235 tost deist ke fust, desvéement
contretrové novelement[1];
més derichief grant joie en[2] ot ke suvent
la dame a lui aval descent.

Aprés deus ans veraiment
240 la vit, mesme le ure, present
a la feste numéement
l'assumptiun, visablement.

A lui parlad asseurement,
e lui demanda tut ducement
245 se suffrir voisist bonement
que ço ke aveit apertement
veu del resuscitement
de sun seint cors, fust a la gent
musstré u nun.—"Bien m'i assent
250 que mustré seit privéement,
nient au puple ki poi attent.

Li siecles a enperement
est turné, pur tant le defenc
ke dit ne seit communement,
255 kar tel le oreit, (ki nien ne i ment),
ki cuntendreit sei folement[3]."

X

Més derichief lui demanda:
"Dame, dunc coment serra
la visiun? coment irra?
260 ja més nuls dunc ne la dira?"
Ele respunt: "Se serra.

La visiun deu la mustera[4]
e par sun angle revela
a tei, e ço te annuncia
265 pur ço k'en tens ki vendera
ne seit retreit a hume ja,

---

[1] ll. 232–236, Trans.: She said nothing, know that I do not lie, for much she feared that evil people, if she had spoken it, would at once have said that it was an invention, a mad thing newly invented.   [2] en is written in above the line.
[3] ll. 252–256, Trans.: the world has deteriorated, therefore I forbid that it should be told in general, for some would hear it (for I do not lie at all) who would behave foolishly.   [4] mustera: 3 sg. preterite of mustrer.

si a celui ki plus me amera,
plus especiament honurra.
Ma loenge tut jurz crestra,
270 e grant bien i avendra,
e cil mut bien l'entendera
ki sen quor a mei desclos a.
A lui mem fiz se desclorra,
e gent gueredun li rendera.
275 Asez de gent recevera
la visiun, e l'entendra
e plus volentiers servira
mum fiz, e mei plus honurra."

XI

Puis la visiun, fu gardée
280 ceste feste, e honurée
mut hautement. Cil ert privé
ki la dame eime de quor lé.
N'est pus se poi nun demuré,
tant cum li prestres ad chanté
285 la messe, a lui est repeiré
la dame; si l'a revisité.
E Ysabel li ad demandé
cumbien en tere ot cunversé
puis ke sen fiz esteit munté;
290 si mesme le an fust presenté
a suen fiz, au ciel mené.
Ele respunt: "N'iert més duté:
de ço un an entier passé
pus ke deus est au ciel turné,
295 ke en tere fu e ai esté.
Tant plus de un an cum est cunté
de la feste ke est numé   Verso 3 f. 95 b
le ascensiun, deske est celebré
l'assumptiun que est apelé,
300 fu en tere vivante leissé
e pus aprés au ciel porté."

XII

E p*us* enq*ui*st s'a sen murir[1]
les apostres tuz venir
i fist deus pur ensevelir
305 le cors, u nu*n*; de ço sentir
que dut, vot de la dame oir.
Ele respunt—ne vot suffrir
s'ancele en dutance cheir—
"Tut i furent p*ur* furnir
310 mes obseq*ui*es e p*ur* se*r*vir,
le cors enterer e enfuir."

XIII

Une autre fiez cum seit[2]
la ancele deu e entendeit
a la dame q*ue* ele soleit
315 tant amer, e chiere aveit,
la feste[3] revenue esteit
q*ua*nt anuntier voleit
sa mere k'il en char vendreit.
La dame, cum ele soleit
320 suvent devant, bien la veeit.
A lui must*r*a sen vut[4] beneit;
ele mut bien le cuniseit,
e de joie q*ue* ele en aveit
p*ri*st hardeme*n*t, si li diseit:
325 "Duce dame, se v*us* pleseit,
mis q*uo*r saveir mut desireit[5]
ma dame cumbien aveit[6]
al tens q*ua*nt li angle veneit
dire q*ue* concevereit
330 le fiz deu, e enfantereit."
E la dame lui responeit
q*ue* cele hure bien saveit.
Quinz anz aveit, e plus esteit
un poi passé. Ki bien estreit
335 trestut le tens i cuntereit,
demi an plus i trovereit.

---

[1] Whether at her death. [2] *seit:* 3 sg. imperfect of *seoir*: was sitting.
[3] March 25th. [4] Her face. [5] Cf. l. 93. [6] l. 327, *Trans.:* how old my lady was.

XIV

Tant anz de la nativité[1],
de la feste ke *est* numé,
le anu*n*ciatiun clamé,
340   q*ua*nt deu lui fu anuncié,
tant pl*us* ke q*ui*nz anz ot passé[2]
q*ua*nt deu conçut ki p*us* fu né,
par ki sumus rechaté
de mort, e d'emfer delivré;
345   ki seit beneit e honuré
sur tute rien ki il ad crié.   Amen.

---

[1] *i.e.* the birthday of the Virgin, September 8th.   [2] Cf. the Latin: "Quindecim, inquit, annos tunc habui, atque insuper tantum temporis, quantum est a commemoratione nativitatis mee usque ad dominice annuntiationis sollempnitatem."

POEM ON THE DAY OF JUDGMENT

EDITED BY H. J. CHAYTOR

INTRODUCTION

THE MS.[1] in which this poem occurs is a volume of 112 pages, containing Excerpta upon religious subjects in handwritings of the first half of the thirteenth century. All are in Latin until this poem is reached; it is followed by the Stabat Mater in Latin and English (Stand wel moder under rode) with a musical setting, which again is followed by a recipe in French, and a prayer in Latin. This poem is written in three columns of 46 lines. The MS. measures $8\frac{1}{2} \times 3$.

The quotation from St Bernard beginning l. 19 is from the *Meditationes devotissimae ad humanae conditionis cognitionem*, caput III, p. 1052 H. in the folio edition of 1620. "Dic mihi, ubi sunt amatores mundi qui ante pauca tempora nobiscum erant? Nihil ex eis remansit, nisi cineres et vermes. Attende diligenter quid sunt, vel quid fuerunt. Homines fuerunt sicut tu, comederunt, biberunt, riserunt, duxerunt in bonis dies suos, et in puncto ad inferna descenderunt (Job xxi, 13). Hic caro eorum vermibus, et illic anima ignibus deputatur.... Ubi risus, ubi jocus, ubi jactantia, ubi arrogantia? De tanta laetitia, quanta tristitia? Post tantillam voluptatem, quam gravis miseria? De illa exultatione ceciderunt in magnam miseriam, in grandem ruinam et in magna tormenta. Quicquid illis accidit, tibi accidere potest, quia homo es.... Certum est quia morieris, sed incertum quando, aut quomodo, vel ubi." The lines preceding the mention of St Bernard are reminiscent of a favourite theme of his. See *De modo bene vivendi*, Sermo IV, de timore Dei. The reference in l. 43 is to Proverbs xi, 4. The description of the Day of Judgment resembles many other medieval poems on the same subject.

The Fifteen Signs of the Day of Judgment, either as forming part of the Gospel of Nicodemus or as treated in isolation, appear in several versions. See Suchier, *Denkmäler provenzalischer Literatur*, Halle, 1883, p. 490, where references are given to most of the literature on this subject. Another version of the Signs of the End of the

---

[1] St John's College, MS. 111, f° 106ʳᵒ.

World, based on the well-known Sibylline acrostics ("judicii signum : tellus sudore madescet"), is found in a poem edited by P. Meyer in the *Bulletin de la Société des anciens textes français*, 1879, p. 74. There was a popular verse translation of the Apocalypse (*Romania*, XXV, p. 200). Many of the numerous moral treatises refer to Hell as an incitement to good conduct. Hence a large number of commonplaces in verse form were available for the use of anyone who needed them. The coincidences between this poem and one in MS. Lambeth, No. 522 (Herrig's *Archiv*, LXIII, p. 67), seem however too numerous to be explained as due to reminiscence. It is difficult to avoid the conclusion that our poet knew the poem of the Lambeth MS., and adapted parts of it to suit his own purposes. The Lambeth poem treats of the birth of Christ (here the MS. is defective) and of the second coming. Compare with l. 71 ff. of our poem the similar passage from the Lambeth poem (l. 17):

Ore oiez ensement
Del secund avenement:
Kar il vendra autre feiz
Al jugement, por tenir dreiz.
Il vint einzceis celeement,
Dunc vendra apertement;
Cil ke juge fu a tort,
Jugera e vifs e mort.
Ceo ert al jur de juyse,
Ou il ert juge e justise,
Jur de grant amerete,
Jur de grant chaitivete,
Jur de ire e de coruz,
Jur de pleynte e de grouz,
Jur de lermes e de plur,
Jur de peyne e de dolur.
   Le solail come sanc avra ruur,
E la lune pale colur;
E le jur ennercira,
E tuit li mund fremira.
Quatre munstres dunc vendrunt
E quatre busines tornerunt[1]
Issi de quatre pars del mund,
Ke cel e terre tremblerunt

---

[1] So editor; a misreading for *cornerunt*?

E tuz les morz releverunt,
Ke unkes furent ou serrunt
Del tens Adam le premerayn
Jeskes al plus tardif dereyn.
De lur tumbes irrunt hors
Chescun od sun propre cors,
Si irrunt ver le jugement
Plurant dolerusement.
　　Dunc vendra nostre seignur...
Od la curt celeste,
Environ lui mult grant tempeste,
E oveke lui turmente grant
E mult orible feu ardant
Ke flammera enmi le vis
Tuit environ ses enemis.

Eight lines later the angels of l. 95 occur:

Les seynz dunc vendrunt
E cel poeple severunt
Chesc*h*un a sun propre degre
Si come le feu les avera pruve.
　　Une partye serrunt a destre,
Autre partye a senestre
Dunc vendra nostre sire avant
Od ses playes tuit sanglant.

Then follows a discourse by Jesus which extends for some 50 lines, and is, together with 160 lines describing the details of the Judgment, compressed by our poet into 36 lines.

There are other points of resemblance between this poem and the Lambeth MS. The latter has a poem (fol. 73) on the transitory nature of earthly things; compare the following with l. 33 of our poem:

Qu'est devenu lur vis rovent,
Lor cors, ke tant fu tel e gent,
Les oilz rianz, li duz parler....

Similarly, the apostrophe to Death finds its counterpart in a long poem (fol. 245) upon the state of the world:

Mort, mult par es cruel, ke tuit vas osciant....

Such commonplaces are, however, of frequent occurrence in the moralising literature of the 14th century.

Amur et pour ad Deu mis

f⁰ 106ʳᵒ col. a

Pur bien garder ses amis.
Pour lur fet lur pechez lesser,
E amur vertuz enbracer.
5   Pour lur fet d'enfer fuir,
E amur lur fet el ceil¹ venir.
Pour, pur veir, ce est la summe
De iii. choses ke neseit² en quer de home.
Ke bien en memorie les ad,
10 Jamés sanz pour ne serat.
Le primer pour est hydur de mort
Ke checun venit e sage e fort;
Riches e poures tretuz devure
E nul ne set ne tens ne le hure.
15 Kar tel est by³ mut grant seynur
Ke en enfer serat devant⁴ le jur;
Tel est huy fort e pussant
Ke demain ert venum puant.
Sein Bernard parout et dit,
20 Si cum nous truvum en sun escrit:
"Di mey, fet il, u sunt la gent
Ke le mund amerent si tendrement,
Ki l'autre jur furent oveke nus
Seyns, heitez e joius?
25 I ad riens de lur char tendre
Fors ord venim e vers e cendre,
Humes furent cum esté vus,
Mangerent e burent oveke nus,
Menoient lur vie en grant delit.
30 E puis en un trés point petit
Dessendirent en abime,
Le alme al fu, la char vermine.
U est ore devenu
Lur ris, lur joie, lur vertu?
35 Pur joye ke amerent taunt,
Ore hunt tritesce e dolur grant,
Chair porid ensement.
Plus tost ke put checun s'amend,
Car certeins sumus⁵ ke morum:

---

¹ ᵉcil: *sic.*   ² which are born *or* <naiser, to mortify.   ³ by, corr. huy.
⁴ deᵘᵃⁿᵗ: "uant" above the line.   ⁵ sum⁹.

40 Coment ne quant, ce ne savum[1]."
   Ky ce pensat, pour averoit,
   E le més[2] de peché se gardereit;
   Car Salemon le sage dit,
   E ses proverbes escrit:
45 " En tuz voz fez, dit il, pensez
   Ta mort e ja ne pecherez."
   O Mort! cum dur e cum amer   (col. b)
   Est ta memorie a verseiller;
   Tu prins ces sodoynement
50 Que quident vivre longement;
   Tu prins les dormans en lur liz,
   Tu tous as riches lur deliz;
   Tu abas en un sul jur
   Li povre e li emperrur[3].
55 Ne est en sicle rien que vive
   Que encontre tei seit postive;
   Tu faz flestri[4] la rose freche;
   Tu fas leiser e jou e treche;
   Tu més devant ce que est derere;
60 Tu prins le fiz avant le pere;
   Tu fas valer e sach e heire
   Autant cum purpre u robe veire.
   Ke vaut honur, ke vaut richese,
   Ke vaut beauté, que vaut hautesse,
65 Quant ceste joie que ci ad
   En un poi d'eure s'en vat?
   Kar ce que joie ici endite,
   Aprés la mort est quite e quite.
   Las! purquei est joie dite
70 Ke de joie nus deserite?
   Ore oiez del jugement
   Dunt pour veint ensement:
   Ce ert el jur de juisse
   Quant Deus meismes ert justise;
75 Jour de lermes et de plurs,
   Jour de peigne e dolur,
   Quant tuz pechez puni serunt,

---

[1] for the spelling -um cf. l. 117.   [2] le més = all the more.   [3] As r is never doubled in this MS., the abbreviation ought perhaps to be expanded as e and not er: corr. therefore "emperur."   [4] (?) Corr. flestrir. Cf. Preface, p. xxiv, Remarks on r.

Quant les esteiles a tere charunt.
Li solail cum sanc devendra,
80   E la lune pale sera,
E jur ennercira,
E tut li mund fremira.
Quatre munstres dunc vendrunt;
De quatre pars del mund irunt;
85   Quatre busines cornerunt,
Que cel e tere trenblerunt.
Idunc vendra le fu ardant
Si orible e si grant
Ki tretuz ardera parmi
90   Que per peché sont rensoili.
E tuz morz releverunt
Ke unkes furent e serunt;
Si irunt vers le jugement   (col. c)
Plurant mut dolurusement.
95   Li seins angles dunc vendrunt
E icel pople departirunt:
La bone gent serunt a destre,
E les chaitifs a senestre.
Dunc vendra nostre seignur auvant
100 O ses plaies tut senglant;
Si vendra tut le mund juger,
Cel, ewe, tere e mer.
Idunc sera tut denostré[1]
Ke unkes fu fet, dit u pensé.
105 Unkes si privé rien ne fu,
Ke apertement ne sera veu,
E qui le fist, quei e coment,
U e quant e come lungement,
Pur quei e ki e comme sovent:
110 Trestut ert veu apertement.
Neporquant de nul peché
Dunt home seit avant purgé
Ne i averat hunte ne pour,
Enz averat joye e honur[2].
115 Dunc demadera[3] nostre seingnur
De tuz les hures del jor

---

[1] Corr. *demostré*.   [2] Yet a man will feel no shame or fear but rather joy and pride about any sins which he may have atoned for previously.   [3] de*mad*era: *sic*.

Coment les aarum¹ usé.

E dunc verum pour verité

Ce que quidum que ore soit bien

120 E que de mal n'eust rien,

Dunc le verum trés led peché

Quant nomement nus ert mustré².

Dunc ne ert pas tens de merci,

Més de plurs, de pleinte e de cri ;

125 Dunc n'er pas tens de penance,

Més de peché dure vengance.

Kar Deus que ore est pacient

Ert dunc irus a mute gent.

O ! quel anguise e quel dolurs

130 Averunt dunc li pecheurs !

Kar il verunt par desus

Deu e ses seins mut irus³ :

Desus les diables tut apert

Enfer contre eus uvert.

135 De einz lur reysun remordant

E tost envirun le mund ardant,

Les diables or unt prestement

Pur mener les en fort torment⁴.

¹ aům : *sic.* The difficulty is to know whether to read "araum" or "aarum." Corr. *averum.* ² And then we shall see in truth what we now think to be good and to have no evil in it, then we shall see it as a very wicked sin when it is shown to us by name. ³ Above them they will see God and his Saints very angry. ⁴ Beneath the devils there appears Hell opened for them. While they regret beforehand their speeches and the world is burning around them, the devils now have permission to lead them into great torment.

DIVISIONES MUNDI

EDITED BY O. H. PRIOR

INTRODUCTION

OUR libraries contain many specimens of a "genre" much cultivated in the Middle Ages: the didactic poem.

Such works were evidently not meant to appeal to the poetic feelings of our ancestors, but they answered another purpose: students were thereby enabled to commit more easily to memory the dry facts of the various sciences. The earliest work of the kind in French is, as far as we know, Philippe de Thaon's *Bestiaire*, describing the various animals. We have likewise poems on stones, on birds, on astronomy, and finally encyclopedias embodying every branch of knowledge, such as *L'Image du Monde*. England is particularly wealthy in works of this kind dealing with single subjects and probably meant to be used in schools where French was the compulsory language, while the Continental French scholar imbibed his science through the medium of Latin.

The *Divisiones Mundi*, written by an unknown author, Perot de Garbelei, is a work of this kind, though, in one important respect, it differs from other didactic poems: it presents dry facts only in as concise a form as possible, without any attempt at drawing moral lessons from descriptions of strange animals in India or elsewhere.

Perot's subject is Geography. He deals briefly with the world in general, the various elements and the division of the earth in three parts, Asia, Africa and Europe. He gives us hardly more than a bare list of names of countries and people, except when he describes the marvels of India, a well worn subject which seems to be inevitable in medieval geographical works.

As an author, Perot does not pretend to be original. He tells us himself that his work is a translation from the Latin, and he cites his source: Isidorus. But here we are forced to differ from him, and to accuse him at least of carelessness. Certain passages, certain names are indeed borrowed from the Spaniard's works, the *Etymologiae*, and others. But the bulk of the *Divisiones* is a direct translation from Honorius Augustodunensis' *De Philosophia Mundi* and *De Imagine Mundi*.

Literal translations from Honorius' Latin are plentiful in our poem and thus many obscure points in the French text can be cleared up. Moreover, although the MS. is written without any division into paragraphs, opposite a certain passage on fol. 402 Perot writes in the margin the abbreviation "N^a": this stands for "Nona," *i.e.* "nine," the number of the chapter in the *Philosophia Mundi* of which it is a translation.

Our author, or his scribe, is very inaccurate as regards names, and riddles offered by certain spellings of towns and countries would be almost insoluble without the help of the Latin version. This is our chief reason for reprinting the original side by side with its translation: it is a help for the understanding of the text and also an interesting example of medieval methods of work.

Perot chose to write his poem in what would correspond to Continental French six-syllable lines. The advantage of such a metre for memorising purposes must have been obvious. Yet we find very few examples of this rhythm in literature. We have Philippe de Thaon's *Bestiaire*, the *Débat du Corps et de l'Ame*, the *Lai du Corn*, the short verses at the end of the laisses in *Guillaume d'Orange*, a certain number of pastourelles, but little besides. This line is used especially in the twelfth century, and is rare in the fourteenth and fifteenth centuries, but comes into use again with the Renaissance.

Thus, in one respect at least, our author showed a certain amount of originality in choosing, at a time when it was unpopular, a metre which best answered his didactic purpose.

We shall probably never know who this author was. Perot de Garbelei has left no trace in literature beyond his *Divisiones Mundi*, and in publishing his poem we are not revealing the work of an unrecognised genius. The poem is interesting from a scientific and linguistic point of view, but not otherwise.

Garbelei, Perot's birthplace or home, is likewise a riddle : no such place is to be found in France or in Great Britain. We have to cross the Irish Channel in order to locate it. And there we have "l'embarras du choix": *bally* is a frequent element in Irish place-names; it originally meant "place" or "situation," its modern meaning is "town" or "townland." *Gar* as a prefix means "short" or "rough."[1] Garbally is the name of several places in Leinster, Munster and Connaught. It appears of course under various spellings : Garbally (King's Co., Co. Galway), Garbolly (Co. Galway), Garvaleh (Co. Clare), etc.

The volume in which our manuscript is found will now provide us with further information. It contains many documents in Latin re-

---

[1] Cf. P. W. Joyce, *Origin and History of Irish Place-names*; P. Woulfe, *Irish Names and Surnames* (Dublin, 1923).

lating to Ireland, such as Papal Bulls, etc., concerning the Brethren of St John of Jerusalem in Ireland, concerning the towns of Waterford and Drogheda ; annals in which many entries, especially amongst the later ones, refer to events in Ireland; a calendar and breviary containing the names of Irish saints. There is also a poem in French on the origin of the Hospitallers and their Rule, which is in the same writing as the *Divisiones*.

It is thus quite evident that the MS. hails from Ireland, and probably from the South. We hope to show later that the *Divisiones* is written in an Anglo-Norman dialect which contains distinctive features of the South, and even more strictly speaking, of the South-West of England. We have here, therefore, a most interesting document, both from a linguistic and social point of view. Another work from Ireland, which may be published later, only confirms our conclusions as regards dialect-features.

The copy of the *Divisiones Mundi* of Perot de Garbelei in the library of Corpus Christi College, Cambridge, is the only one known to be in existence. It almost fills 32 pages (fo. 394–fo. 425) of a volume which is thus described by Dr M. R. James in his *Descriptive Catalogue of the Manuscripts in the Library of Corpus Christi College, Cambridge*, 1912, Vol. II, page 286: "No. 405, Chartae, Liturgica, Poemata, etc.... Vellum, $8\frac{7}{10} \times 5\frac{4}{8}$, ff. 1–253, several volumes of cent. XIII and XIV early, all well written. Evidently belonged to the brethren of St John of Jerusalem at Waterford. Contents....28. *Divisiones Mundi* (autore Perot de Garbelai) p. 394."

The writing and linguistic features of our MS. indicate the beginning of the fourteenth century as the probable date of its composition.

The versification is typical of the Anglo-Norman dialect, and illustrates most of the points with which we have dealt in the Preface. The lines are to be scanned with *three* accented or stressed syllables, *e.g.*:

l. 1. Un lívre dé haut évre.

l. 15. Taunt né saverêit de léttre.

l. 17. En románce né rimér.

l. 18. Tant né saverêit limér.

l. 23. E dé clers é de laîs.

l. 26. Kúer éntendánz.

REFERENCES

Pliny, *Opera* (ed. J. Sillig, Hamburg, 1851).

Honorius Augustodunensis, *Opera* (Migne, *Patrologia*, Vol. 172).

Isidorus, *Opera* (Migne, *Patrologia*, Vols. 81–84).

Gossouin, *L'Image du Monde* (ed. O. H. Prior, Paris, 1913). In this edition the question of origins is fully dealt with.

HIC INCIPIU*N*T DIVISIONES MU*N*DI

Honorius Augustodunensis,
De Imagine Mundi Libri Tres.

p.394 Un livre de haut evre
    Ki descrist e deskevre
    Les choses de ceo mund
    E les gens ki i sunt
5   A je en cunte trové.
    Meint bon clerc ben fundé
    E de clergi eslit
    Ferment preisent ceste livre[1].
    E[2] foundé de clergie
10 Ki le lisent ou manie,
    Kar tute est en latin
    Del chef deck en la fin.
    Plusurs clers dient[3] ben
    Ke nul pour nule ren,
15 Taunt ne savereit de lettre,
    Ne purreit mie mettre
    En romance ne rimer,
p.395 Tant ne savereit limer.
    Pur ceo s'en est par fei
20 Perot de Garbelei
    Entremis, pur aver
    Le gré e le voler
    E de clers e de lais,
    Kar requide ke unke més
25 Ne fu fet tel romanz.
    Kuer entendanz
    Merveilles i orra
    Dunt se merveillera.
    De tute creature
30 I orrez la nature.
    Dit v*us* serra brevement
    Ki sunt li element
    Dunt nus tuz furmez sumes,
    Fors le espirit k'evoumes.

---

[1] ? corr. "escrit," or there may be omission of at least 2 lines between ll. 7 and 8.   [2] =est, cf. ll. 83, 314, 619, 860.   [3] *t* above the line.

35 Kant l'uevre ai envaie,
Deu apele en aie,
E le seint espirit,
Ke a finir me ait.
Veritez e resun
40 Dunt ceo livre fesum
Nus dit ben e aporte,
Testemoigne e enorte,
Ke primes est en ce livre[1].
Devum le mund descrivre
45 Quel il est, pur saveir
La porté e l'aveir.
Li mund est, c'est la soume,

p. 39 6 Rounz cum une poume.
De l'ef a la semblaunce
50 Par dreit devisaunce[a].
Si *vus* dirrai brevement
En quele guise e coment:
L'ef est, iceo savez,
D'eskale virounez[b].
55 E pus, aprés l'eskale
Est li aubes, sans faille[c].
L'ordre si est iteus
Ke aprés est li moiels[d].
Einz au moiel s'amasse
60 Une gute mut grasse;
C'est le germeine de l'ef[a e]:
A verité le preuf.
De l'ef *vus* ai mustré,
Par resun e verité:
65 Del mund orrez mustrance
Par itel semblaunce.
Issi cum l'ef, sanz faille,
Est enclose de l'escaille,
Issi porcent le mund,
70 Si cum il est round,
Del cel, ce sachet ben,
Mar doterez de ren[f].

[a] "Li mund...devisaunce."
LIBER I. CAP. I.—Mundus...Hujus figura est in modum pilae rotunda. Sed instar ovi elementis distincta.

[b] "L'ef...virounez."
Ovum quippe exterius testa undique ambitur,

[c] "E pus...faille."
testae albumen,

[d] "L'ordre...moiels."
albumini vitellum,

[e] "Einz...de l'ef."
vitello gutta pinguedinis includitur.

[f] "Issi cum l'ef...de ren."
Sic mundus undique coelo, ut testa, circumdatur,

---

[1] Veritez...livre: Truth and reason, with which we compose this book, tell us and report, testify and teach what is found for the first time in this book.   [2] Cf. 1. 95 etc.

La firmament desuz[1],
Ki esteilé est tuz,

75 Del cel est ceint e clos,
En verité dire l'os[2],
Si cum l'abuns ceo est

p. 397 Ke tut le clot e vest[g].
Le firmament lerrai

80 E de l'eir parlerai
Ke veum veirement
E trouble e cler sovent.
Del firmament e[3] ceint,
Ke del[4] esteiles est paint[5].

85 L'eir aseint entresait
Si cum li aubuns fait
Le moel e enclot,
Ne vus en ment d'un mot[6h].
Dreit est ke vus desire[7]

90 Coment vet de la tere :
L'eir, sachez sanz dute,
La ceint e enclot tute,
Si cum li moels fait
Le germe entresait[i].

95 Issi cum de cel germe[8]
Nest a ure ne a terme
Li poucinet furmez,
Si nest e fruit e blez
De tere e de autre chose,

100 Si cum li livre glose.
Fet avum mostrement
Par bref ordeinement
Del mund e quei en chet,
Quel est e cum il set[j].

105 Ore vus covent entendre,
Si vus voleth aprendre
Coment nus sumes fet

p. 398 E de quele chose estreit[9]:

[g] "La firmament...vest."
coelo vero purus aether ut album,

[h] "Le firmament...d'un mot."
aetheri turbidus aer, ut vitellum,

[i] "L'eir...Le germe entresait."
aeri terra, ut pinguedinis gutta
includitur.

[j] "Issi cum...e cum il set" (*not in Honorius*).
"Ex vitello autem et albugine
ovi constat pullum in eo formari
et nasci ;
et ex terra vel aqua cuncta pro-
duci ac formari animantia liber
iste commemorat.
...ut inde postmodum hominem
et animantia caetera quasi de ovo
pullum formaret..."
(Abelardus, *Expositio in Hexae-
meron*, in Migne, *Patrologia*,
Vol. 178, col. 736 A and B.)

---

[1] Hon. I, lxxxvii, "Superius coelum dicitur firmamentum,...stellis undiqueversum ornatum"; cf. also l. 84.   [2] I dare say it in truth.   [3] =est.   [4] Corr. *d'*.
[5] Cf. l. 73 note.   [6] L'eir...mot: *the firmament* surrounds the air just as the white of the egg does in the case of the yolk which it encloses.   [7] Corr. *desere*; *dessere*=développer, exposer.   [8] Cf. l. 61.   [9] Cf. Hon. *De phil. mundi*, I, xxi, *De elementis*; Isid., *Etym.* XIII, iii, 3 ; Gen. ii, 7.

Sachet certeinement
110 Ke sunt .iiii. element.
Li primer est li feus.
L'autre est l'air ça jus.
Li tierce, k'emfassez,
Ceo est l'ewe, ceo sachez.
115 E li quars, c'est tere
A ki le cors repeire.
Ces .iiii. choses ci
Ke jeo vus nome e di
Se comencent ensemble,
120 Si cum pur veir me semble.
L'un si a veirement
De l'autre atemprement[1].
Le fu est chaud e secks
E li air chaud e frés:
125 Frés, di je, pur l'ummur
Ki est od la chalur.
Humour est moistez,
La resun en oez:
L'eve i[2] est, cum me semble,
130 E freide e moiste ensemble.
Ben ceo conois e vei
Ke la tere a en sei
E freidour e secheté.
Ore oi[3] la verité
135 Des elemens escrit
E lur nature dit.
p. 399 Ore oez cum chescune
Est a l'autre commune,
E cum feitement
140 Ens sunt ovelement
Entre eus enlaciez
E ensemble liez:
La tere freide e seche
Ki en sei se deseche,
145 Au fu si va liant
Pur la secheté grant
Ki li uns e l'autre a.

k "Sachet…a la tere joint."
Honorius. LIBER I. CAP. III.—
*De quatuor elementis. Elementa
unde dicantur. Quot sint elementa; quomodo invicem miscean-
tur. Situs elementorum.*
Elementa…ex quibus constant
omnia, scilicet, ignis, aer, aqua,
terra. Quae in modum circuli in
se revolvuntur, dum ignis in
aerem, aer in aquam, aqua in
terram convertitur, rursus terra
in aquam, aqua in aerem, aer in
ignem commutatur. Haec singula
propriis qualitatibus, quasi qui-
busdam brachiis se invicem tenent, et discordem sui naturam
concordi foedere vicissim com-
miscent.

Nam terra arida et frigida fri-
gidae aquae connectitur; aqua
frigida et humida humido aeri
astringitur; aer humidus et calidus
calido igni associatur; ignis calidus et aridus aridae terrae copulatur.

---

[1] One is tempered by the other.   [2] *i* above the line.   [3] Corr. *ai.*

De ces .ii. issi va:
Li fu e li autre sunt
150 De chalour ki unt
Ambedui lié ensemble,
Li uns a l'autre ensemble,
Issi pur la[1] chalour.
E li eir, pur l'umur
155 Ke il l'eve rent,
A lui se lie e prent.
De l'ewe ne ment mie:
A la tere se lie
E enlace e enprent.
160 Pur la freidur ki vent
De deu parz itel pouint,
L'ewe a la tere joint[*].
Ki[2] par numbre veut quere
L'espace de la tere,
165 Issi le poet saver
E le dreit cunte aver,
p.400 Si Ysidres[3] ne ment
Ki par dreit provement
Parla del mund asez,
170 Cum il est cumpassez;
Mult par en sout e vit,
Si en fist un escrist
Dunt cist livre est faiz
E en romanz escraiz[4].
175 Si vus vint a talent,
Ore oiez pleinement
Kantes lieus poez fere
La ceinte de la tere:
Mil millers fere deit
180 Par .xii. fiez tut dreit
E .l. ii. pus,
Si cum en livre truis .
Estre deivent oies
Queus sunt les .iii. parties

[l]"Ore oiez…truis."
LIBER I. CAP. V.—Circuitus autem terrae, centum et octoginta millibus stadiorum mensuratur, quod duodecies mille milliaria, et quinquaginta duo computatur….

[m]"Estre…afiche."
LIBER I. CAP. VII.—Habitabilis

---

[1] lla (*sic*), first *l* slightly below line.   [2] K large initial.   [3] Cf. Bozon, p. 8, No. 1, Le noble clerk Ysidre…; p. 135, No. 117, …sicom dit Ysidre (*Les contes moralités de Nicole Bozon*, ed. L. Toulmin Smith et P. Meyer, *Société des Anciens Textes Français*, Paris, 1889).   [4] Corr. *estraiz.*

185 Del mund pur quei *vus*
    plaisie.
    La p*ri*mere est Asie
    Ke de maint ben habunde;
    Europe est la secunde;
    E la terce est Aufrike,
190 Cum verité l'afiche*ᵐ*.
    La primere cuntré
    E ce ke Asie est apelé
    Si se espant e estent
    Tresparmi l'orient
195 Dreske endreit medi*ⁿ*.
    En d'iluec, ce *vus* di,
p.401 Aufrike si s'estent
    Dekes en occident.
    De occident se reva
200 Europe par dela,
    Tut en avironant
    Vers le solail levaunt*ᵒ*.
    Primes deit estre oie
    La primere partie
205 Del mund, cum ele va,
    Queus teres il i a.
    Des ewes de la mere[1]
    I orrez deviser,
    E de bestes e de genz
210 Ki i sunt manant enz.
    La dient ke deit estre
    Le parais terestre.
    Mult par est covenables
    Cel lu, et delitables.
215 Nul n'i vait[2] aler houme
    Cele part, ceo est la soume.
    Clos est de mur, sanz fable,
    Tut a feu resemblable,
    De ci k'as cels en sume[3]:
220 Ni puet aler nus home*ᵖ*.
    La est l'arbre de vie.
    Verité testemonie,

zona, quae a nobis incolitur in tres partes Mediterraneo mari dirimitur. Quarum una Asia, altera Europa, tertia Africa dicitur.

ᵐ"La primere...medi."
Asia a septentrione per orientem, usque ad meridiem; Europa ab occidente usque ad septentrionem;

ᵒ"Aufrike...levaunt."
Africa a meridie usque ad occidentem extenditur.

ᵖ"La dient...nus home."
LIBER I. CAP. VIII.—Asia... Hujus prima regio in oriente e paradiso; locus videlicet omni amoenitate conspicuus, inadibilis hominibus, qui igneo muro usque ad coelum est cinctus.

ʳ"La est...savereit."
LIBER I. CAP. IX.—In hoc lig-

---

[1] Corr. *mer*, cf. l. 881.   [2] =voit.   [3] Clos...sume: truthfully it is enclosed with a wall-like fire which extends from here to heaven.

Ki del fruit mang*e*reit
Jammés ne murreit.
225 De celui ne gusta
Adam, kaunt trespassa
p.402 La Deu obedience,
Més le fruit de science.
Cel fruit itel esteit
230 Ke mal e ben savereit[1]ʳ.
En icele paradis
Ke jeo *vus* ci devis
La est une funteine,
Ceo est chose certeine;
235 De ilokes nest e sort,
Par desuz tere curt[2].
De la funteine venent
Quatre[3] fluies ke tene*n*t
Lur curs e lur repeire
240 Mult loinz e par meinte tereˢ.
Des fluvies *vus* sei dire
E lur nouns descruire.
Li uns a nun Phison
E li secunde Gyson;
245 Le terce *vus* devis,
Celi a nun Tygris;
E li quarte en aprés
Ad nun Eufratés.
Li livres nus espont
250 Ke en Inde a un gr*a*nt mont.
Ben sai nomer sun non:
Orgobanés out non.
De cest mont est issaunt
Phison cel fluie grant.
255 Oiez de l'autre fluie,
Ceo ke veirs en espreue[4].
p.403 Just un mont nest en bas,
E si ad non Athas.
L'ewe clot e enserre.

num vitae, videlicet arbor de cujus fructu qui comederit, semper in uno statu immortalis permanebit.

ˢ "En icele...meinte tere."
In hoc etiam fons oritur, qui in quatuor flumina dividitur. Quae quidem flumina infra paradisum terra conduntur;

sed in aliis longe regionibus funduntur.
ᵗ "Des fluvies ... Armanie est apelé.
Liber I. Cap. X.—*De quatuor fluminibus. Physon sive Ganges, Geo sive Nilus, Tigris, Euphrates.*

Nam Physon, qui et Ganges in India de monte Orcobares nascitur, et contra orientem fluens Oceano excipitur.

Geon, qui et Nilus juxta montem Athlantem surgens, mox a terra absorbetur,

---

[1] De celui...savereit. Cf. Genesis iii, 1–6.   [2] Cf. l. 260.   [3] In margin capital N with small *a* above it.   [4] Corr. *espruie*? or cf. 850–1, *flueve*: *preve*. The better correction would be: *flueve*: *espreve*.

260 Si decurt par desuz tere.
   Pleinement sun curs a ;
   Au rivage s'en va
   De la Ruge Mer dreit,
   E de ilukes endreit
265 Par Egypte s'empaint,
   Si ke Ethiope ençaint.
   Par cest[1] curs fet s'issue,
   K'el vet, home par veue[2],
   En la *gr*ant mer espandre
270 Lez la grant Alixandre.
   Tigris e Eufratés
   Si courent a eslés
   En une grant cuntré.
   Armanie est apelé'.
275 Aprés paradis a
   Main[3] desert ke ja
   Ne serrunt habité,
   Tant la *gr*ant plenté
   De bestes e de serpenz
280 Ke sunt conve*r*sant de-
   denz".
   Aprés ces desertines,
   Od tant ad sauvagines,
   Si est Inde la grans.
284 Aprés est Occeans,
p.404 Une mer grant e lée,
   Ke issi est apelé.
   En ceo mer la
   Une grant idle i a
   Ke a noun Taprolainne.
290 De .x. cités est plainne,
   Burkes e viles ovec[v].
   Les gens ki sunt iluec[4]
   Grant sunt outre mesure.
   Itel est lur nature
295 Ke vivent lungement.

per quam occulto meatu currens,

in littore Rubri maris denuo funditur,
Aethiopiam circumiens per Aegyptum labitur, in septem ostia divisus, magnum mare juxta Alexandriam ingreditur.

Tigris autem et Euphrates in Armenia de Monte Barchoatro funduntur, et contra meridiem vergentes Mediterraneo mari junguntur.

   u"Aprés paradis...dedenz."
Post paradisum sunt multa loca deserta et invia, ob diversa serpentum et ferarum genera.

   v"Aprés ces desertines...viles ovec."
LIBER I. CAP. XI.—Deinde est India ab Indo flumine dicta. Qui ad Septentrionem de monte Caucaso nascitur, et ad meridiem cursum suum dirigens, a Rubro mari excipitur. Hoc India ab occidente clauditur, et ab hoc Indicus oceanus dicitur. In quo etiam est sita Taprobanes insula, decem civitatibus inclyta.
   w"Les gens ki...au muntant."
(*Not in Honorius.*)
Pliny VI, xxii, 24[5]. "Ultra montis

---

[1] Corr. *set*, *i.e.* seven.   [2] In the sight of man.   [3] Corr. *maint*. Cf. ll. 6, 734, 766, 897.   [4] ll. 292–308 describe the Seres. Cf. also Isid., *Etym.* XIV, iii, 29, "...caeterarum gentium commercia abnuentes Seres,..."   [5] Pliny, *Naturalis Historiae Libri xxxvii* (ed. J. Sillig, Hamburg, 1851, Vol. I, p. 434).

Nus lur langage n'entent
Ne il autre ne entendent
Kant achatent ou vendent
Nul marchandise.
300 Ore oez en quele guise
Marchandise funt,
Kant autre gent i unt.
A lur rivage tendent
Lur aveir e atendent.
305 Teus cum volent aver
Pernent a lur voler;
De lur repernent tant,
S'il rendent au muntant[1]^w.
Cele gent ki la sunt
310 .ij. yvers en l'an unt,
E .ij. estez ausi,
Ceo sachez ben de fi.
Tote la tere entur
p.405 E[2] tut tens en vedur[3].
315 La sunt li mun d'or plein,
De ceo seez ben certeinc,
Més tant dragouns i a
Ke nul n'ose aler la^x.
Liuns[4] Inde est parant
320 Caspius, un mont grant.
Procheins est de une mer
Ke en romanz oi nomer
La mer de Caspe dreit,
Kar del mund mult receit[5];
325 Del mund est issi dite.
Une gent i habite:
Goz e Magoz unt nun.
Cruel sunt e felun.
Ilokes enclos sunt
330 De la mer e de la[6] mund.
Nul ne poet fors aler,
Ne nul a eus entrer.

Emodos, Seras quoque ab ipsis adspici, notos etiam conmercio; patrem Rachiae conmeasse eo, advenis sibi Seras occursare. Ipsos vero excedere hominum magnitudinem, rutilis comis, caeruleis oculis, oris sono truci, nullo conmercio linguae. Cetera eadem, quae nostri negotiatores. Fluminis ulteriore ripa mercis positas juxta venalia tolli ab his, si placeat permutatio, non aliter odio justiore luxuriae...."

^{x} "Cele gent...aler la."
Honorius. LIBER I. CAP. XI.—
Haec duas aestates et duas hiemes uno anno habet, et omni tempore viret. In hoc etiam Chrisa et Argare insulae, auro et argento fecundae et semper floridae. Ibi sunt et montes aurei, qui propter dracones et gryphes non possunt adiri.

^{y} "Liuns...manere sunt."
In India est mons Caspius, a quo Caspium mare vocatur.

Inter quem et mare Gog et Magog ferocissimae gentes,

---

[1] A description of "dumb trading" is already found in Herodotus. This custom is attested by travellers in Northern Africa even in the fifteenth century. [2] =est. [3] (?) Corr. verdur. Cf. Preface, p. xxiv, Remarks on r. [4] Corr. lians. [5] For it receives much (water) from the mountain. [6] Corr. del mund, cf. ll. 320, 324, 325.

La de ilokes enclot,   a magno Alexandro inclusae fe-
O tut sun *grant* ost,   runtur.
335   Alisaundre ki fist
Tanz beuz e tant cumquist.
La char de home manguent   Quae humanis carnibus vel crudis
E de bestes k'il tuent: bestiis vescuntur.
Ja quire nel quirunt[1].
340   A tele manere sunt[y].
Entre *vus* deit mustré[2]   [a] "Entre vus...a la nue."
Ke en Inde, par verité,   India habet quadraginta quatuor
I a quatre cuntrées   regiones, populosque multos, Gar-
p. 406   E quatre beu pueplés.   manos, Orestas, Coatras,
345   Diverse gent i sunt.
Laienz mut en parfunt
Sunt une gent manant;
Si unt a nun Garmant.
E li Coatriem,
350   E li Orestien,
L'i mainent a delivre,
Si cum trovu*m* a livre
Ke ne ment ne ne faut.
Si la sunt si trés[3] haut
355   Kes[4] bois ke par veue   quorum sylvae tangunt aethera.
Adeissent[5] a la nue[x].
Cele part, as montagnes,   [a] "Cele part...vii anz."
I a une gens loigtaines;   In montanis Pygmaeos duorum
Pigemeins les nome   cubitorum homines, quibus bel-
360   Le livre, ce est la some.   lum est contra grues, qui tertio
Ices gens n'ont tretutes   anno pariunt, octavo senescunt.
De longour fors .iii. cothes.
A grues se cumbatent
K'en lur tere s'enbatent.
365   De tele nature sunt
Ke en treis anz enfanz unt,
E en .vii. evillissent
E de lur juvence issent:
Si lur est en .vii. anz[a].
370   La creist de pevre blancs;   [b] "La creist...froncist."

---

[1] Ja...quirunt: never will they cook it.   [2] (?) Corr. *mustrer*. Cf. Preface,
p. xxiv, Remarks on *r*.   [3] treis (*sic*).   [4] Corr. *les*.   [5] a (*in margin*)
Deissent (*sic*).

Més mult i ad de serpens
Es arbreilles laienz.
Oez cum les aturment[1]:
p.407 La gent ki i sejornent
375 Iloec venent; si jettent
Le fu; és rams i mettent.
Li serpent tut li s'en corent,
Pur le chaud nie demerent.
Le pevre si vertist,
380 De la chalur froncist[5].
En cel tere la
Une tele gent i a:
Grant sunt outre resun.
Maanciem unt a nun;
385 N'en saiez ja dotant,
.xii. cotes de grant
Unt tele gent, sanz faille.
As grifuns funt bataille,
Une oiseauz granz e forz,
390 Ke de leon unt corz.
E les ungles ke unt
Semblable a egle sunt[c].
Une gent la i habite
Ki unt nun Agroite.
395 En autre lu converse
Une mult gent[2] diverse
A ceus dunt ai parlé:
Baramain sunt apelé.
Ben vus dirrai de ceus,
400 Quel nature unt entre eus:
E le[3] fu ardaunt se launcent
Si ferement s'avauncent
Lur vie e lur veillesce,
p.408 E rechangent en jovenesce[d].
405 La resunt autre gent
Ku tuent lur parent,
Kant enveillez turnent[5].

Apud hos crescit piper colore
quidem albo: sėd cum ipsi serpentes, qui ibi abundant, flamma
fugantur, nigrum colorem trahit
de incendio.

[c]"En cel tere...egle sunt."
Item Macrobios duodecim cubitorum longos, qui bellant contra
gryphes, qui corpora leonum,
alas et ungulas praeferunt aqui-
larum.

[d]"Une gent la...jovenesce."
Item Agroctas

et Bragmanos,

qui se ultro in ignem mittunt
amore alterius vitae.

[e]"La resunt...creire."
Sunt alii qui parentes jam senio
confectos mactant,

---

[1] Corr. *aturnent*.   [2] Cf. for this construction with " mult " l. 658.
[3] Corr. *El* (or, *en le*).   [4] If they feel themselves getting dangerously old, they
throw themselves in a blazing fire and become young again.   [5] Kant...turnent:
when they become (turn) old.

Sil quisent e afornent
Pur manger sanz retraire.
410 E ke ceo ne veut fere
Entre eus est mal venu ;
Pur traiture est tenu.
Gens autre i a estrange
Ke de ces mult se chaunge.
415 Les peissuns tut cruz usent.
Taunt ne kaunt ne refu-
sent
La mer salé a bevre¹:
De veir le poez creire*.
Autre genz i sunt
420 Ke meins a reburs unt,
E .viii. orteus és pez.
Si resunt, ceo sachez,
Uns autres genz lointaine
Ki testes unt de chene.
425 Mult lunges e corvés sunt
Les ungles ke és deis unt.
Nul de eus n'est ki ja veste
Si del pel nun de beste².
Issi cum chen abaient*.
430 A tele nature traient
La femme kaunt ele efante,
Ki me fest creante
Li livre ki le dit
p.409 E pur veir le descrit.
435 Tut nesent veirent³
Chanu icele gent.
Si sachez ben de veir
Ke en veillesce sunt neir,
E vivent plus asez
440 De nus, ceo est veritez*.
Autres femmes le hantent
Ke par .v. fez emfaunt-
ent.

et eorum carnes ad epulandum
parant,
isque impius judicatur, qui hoc
facere abnegat.

Sunt alii

qui pisces ita crudos edunt,

et salsum mare bibunt.

ᶠ"Autre genz...abaient."
LIBER I. CAP. XII.—...sunt ii
qui aversas habent plantas, et
octonos simul sedecim in pedibus
digitos, et alii, qui habent canina
capita, et ungues aduncos,

quibus est vestis pellis pecudum,

et vox latratus canum.
ᵍ"A tele nature...veritez."
Ibi etiam quaedam matres semel
pariunt, canosque partus edunt,
qui in senectute nigrescunt, et
longa nostrae aetatis tempora
excedunt.

ʰ"Autres femmes...cum bestes."
Sunt aliae, quae quinquennes
pariunt :

---

¹ The MS. has "beure": perhaps we might read "beiire." there are none but clothe themselves in the skins of beasts. ² Nul...beste : ³ Corr. *veirement*.

.v. fiez portent enfanz,
Més ne vivent ke .viii. anz[1].

445 Gent i a de rechef
Ki n'unt ke une oil el chef.
Si resunt une gent
Ki unt nun verraiement
Li Arimaspine ;

450 Autre, Ciclopiene.
Une gent redivise
De merveillus guise ;
Grant merveil est de ceus
Ke une pé i ad chescuns.

455 De une launce s'apuient.
Plus tost corent et fuient
Ke cheval acorsez.
Sachez ceo est veritez :
Une autre gent resunt

460 Ke nule teste n'unt.
De ceus mentir ne voil ;
Savez ou sunt lur oil ?
Es espaules en unt ;

p.410 Car trous el piz unt,

465 Tut pur nés e pur bouche.
Par unt l'alloine touche[2].
Icele gent sanz testes
Velus sunt cum bestes[k].
De autre gent vus dirrai

470 E les vus descruerai[3].
Prochen sunt, ce m'est
    avis,
Del fluie de Gandis.
La creissent une pomes
Dunt ben parler devums.

475 De l'odur sulement
En vivent cele gent.
Grant vertu unt e fort.
Nul ne vet ren ke n'em port[4],

sed partus octavum annum non
excedunt.
Ibi sunt et monoculi,

et Arimaspi,
et Cyclopes.

Sunt et Scinopodae, qui uno tantum fulti pede

auram cursu vincunt, et in terram
positi umbram sibi planta pedis
erecta faciunt.
Sunt alii absque capite,

quibus sunt oculi in humeris,

pro naso et ore duo foramina in
pectore,

setas habent ut bestiae.

[i]"De autre...porteient."
Sunt alii juxta fontem Gangis
fluvii,

qui solo odore cujusdam pomi
vivunt,

qui si longius eunt, pomum secum

---

[1] Cf. Isid., *Etym.* xi, iii, 27, "Perhibent et in eadem India esse gentem feminarum, quae quinquennes concipiunt, et octavum vitae annum non excedunt." [2] Par...touche: they have a very sweet breath. This detail is missing both in Isidorus and Honorius. [3] Corr. *descriverai.* [4] Nul...port: none of them go any distance without carrying some (apples).

Kar autrement moreient,

480   Si ovec eus n'em porteient*.

Iloec sunt habitant

Serpenz issi trés grant

Ke les teres[1] tuz devourent

E les femmes acorent.

485   Une beste maint la

Ke a noun Ceutrocata.

Merveille est grant e fors,

Ane semble de cors ;

Piz a par divisiun,

490   E quises de liun.

Tel est, de fei, aval,

E pez ad de cheval.

Une corn en la teste

p.411 Ad icele fere beste;

495   Bouche a merveille grant;

Voiz de home a par sem-
          blant*.

Iloec i est veue

Une beste corsue ;

En romanz autre trové

500   K'en la nome Ealé.

Fere est e mult fet mal.

Del cors semble cheval,

De cowe, olifaunt.

El front porte devant

505   .ij. cornes ke grant sunt.

L'un d'eles respunt

Derere sun cors tute ;

De l'autre fert e boute

Kant il est en irour.

510   Dunke a neir la colur*.

La sunt li tort[2] tut bloi ;

Pur verité dire l'oi ;

Colur unt de menvers,

E mult orrible cheres.

515   Les goules unt baés,

Deske as oreilles leés.

---

ferunt : moriuntur enim si pravum odorem trahunt.

*"Iloec sunt...par semblant."

LIBER I. CAP. XIII.—Sunt ibi serpentes tam vasti, ut cervos devorent, et ipsum etiam Oceanum transnatent. Ibi est bestia Ceucocroca,

cujus corpus asini, clunes cervi,

pectus et crura leonis,

pedes equi,
ingens cornu bisulcum, vastus oris hiatus usque ad aures...*In loco dentium, os solidum*, vox pene hominis.

*"Iloec i est...la colur."

Ibi est alia bestia Eale,

cujus corpus equi, *maxilla Apri*, cauda elephantis,

cubitalia cornua habens, quorum unum post tergum reflectit, cum alio pugnat. *Illo obtuso, aliud ad certamen vibrat.*

Nigro colore horret. *In aqua et in terra aequaliter valet.*

*"La sunt li tort ... unt de cheval."

Ibi sunt fulvi tauri, versis setis horridi, grande caput,
oris rictus ab aure ad aurem patet....

---

[1] Corr. *ceres* = cers.   [2] Corr. *tor.*

Ne lur poet home mal fere,   Omne missile duro tergo re-
Ne point de sank atrere   spuunt....
E espée ne quarraus,
520 Tant unt dures les peaus.
Autre beste ilokes a   Ibi quoque Mantichora bestia,
Ke a nun Manticora.
Ben est dreit ke le sace :
p.412 Home resemble de face.   facie homo,
525 De .iii. pez a les denz.   triplex in dentibus ordo,
Si mangue les genz.
De cors semble lioun ;   corpore leo,
De cowe, scorpioun.   cauda scorpio, oculis glauca,
Cruel est a merveille.
530 Cum sanc est vermeille.   colore sanguinea,
Sifle de serpent a,   vox sibilus serpentum,
E plus cort e va   fugiens discrimina volat, velocior
Ke oisel ne poet voler.   cursu quam avis volatu, humanas
Iloec i a, sanz doter,   carnes habens in usu.
535 Buels[1] de mult grant vertu,   Ibi sunt etiam boves tricornes,
De .iii. cornes cornu.
Ne sai li[2] funt nul mal,
Més pez unt de cheval'.   pedes equinos habentes.
Autre beste converse   *m* "Autre beste...de ber non."
540 Ilokes mult diverse.   Ibi quoque monoceros, cujus
Pur verité dire l'os   corpus equi,
Ke ad nun Monoceros.
Veirs est de cele beste
Cerf semble de la teste,   caput cervi,
545 E del chef en aval
Semble cors de cheval,
E del piz[3] oliphant,   pedes elephantis,
Mult i sunt resemblant.
De la cowe derere   cauda suis :
550 E[4] de porc la mennere.
Un corn mult grant   Uno cornu, in medio fronte ar-
A enz le frount devant ;   matum
Si est ben, se sachez,
p.413 Lunge entur .iiii. peez[5];   quatuor pedum longo,

---

[1] Corr. *Buefs.*   [2] ? Corr. *si.*   [3] ? Corr. *pez,* cf. l. 538 and Hon. "cujus...
pedes elephantis...."   [4] *e* = est.   [5] Corr. *pez,* cf. ll. 492, 525, 538 etc.

555 Ague est durement   splendenti et mire acuto....
    E si resplent clerement;
    Tele est cum je devis.
    El fluie de Gangis   In Gange quoque sunt anguillae
    Uns angules sunt
560 Ki, par verité, unt   trecentorum pedum longae.
    Trente pez de lungur.
    E ilokes entour   Ibi etiam quidam vermes,
    Sunt un vermesel gr*a*nt;
    De chen unt le semblant   qui instar cancri bina habent
565 E si¹ cotes de braz.   brachia, sex cubitorum longa,
    A mescrere ne faz:
    Les oliphanz oscient   quibus elephantes corripiunt et
    E és ewes, ce dient,   undis immergunt.
    Lur conv*er*sement tenent.
570 Dunt ce en la mer venent   Indicum quoque mare gignit tes-
    Un mult grant limaçon.   tudines,
    Del teste² funt lur mesun   de quarum testis capacia hospitia
    La gent de la cuntrée,   sibi faciunt homines.
    Verité est prové.
575 En Inde le grant   India quoque magnetem lapidem
    Une pere aimant   gignit,
    Si fer touche ne vent³,   qui ferrum rapit.
    Li fer tuz jours se tent
    Ke il ne se poet estuerre⁴.
580 La pere est de tel ordre: Adamantem etiam, qui non nisi
    Froisé ne la poet l'om   hircino sanguine frangi potest.
    Si par le sanc de ber⁵
    non*ᵐ*.
    Des gens avez arere
p.414 Oiez la manere⁶,
585 De bestes ensement.
    Oier purreth brevement
    Des cuntrés les nouns,
    Si cum nus les dirruns,
    Pus ke oir les volés.
590 Un mons a gr*a*ns e lez   ᵐ"Un mons...ke la prent."

---

¹ Corr. *sis*.   ² Corr. *test*.   ³ Une pere...vent: If the loadstone
touches or comes to iron....   ⁴ Corr. *estordre*.   ⁵ Corr. *her(c)*, Lat.
hircum.   ⁶ Des gens...manere: You have heard above about the various kinds
of people.

Utre Inde mult en sus,
E si a nun Indus[1].
De li est apelé
Inde la grant cuntré.
595 De ceste mont ke[2] est si
grant
Parta une tere grant
Decke al fluie de Tygris[3]
Dunt devaunt vus descris[4],
Si cum verité touche.
600 Aprés est Aragote;
E pus i est Assire
Dunt Assur fu tut sire;
Pur Assur nomé
Assure[5] la cuntré.
605 Fiz Seim fu Assur,
De ceo seez seur.
Aprés est Mede e Perse
Ou mainte gent converse.
En Perse la cuntrée
610 Fu primes l'art trové
Pur quei hom enfomente.
La est, sanz ke ne mente,
Une pere petite
p.415 K'en apele perite[6];
615 La maint[7] art e esprent
De celui ke la prent[?].
De Tygrés[8] en aprés
Desike Eufratés
E[9] Mesopothanie,
620 Une garnie[10].
La a une cité
Ke a nun Ninivé;
.iij. jours a dec[11] errure,
Ceo est verité, tant dure.

LIBER I. CAP. XIV.—Ab Indo
flumine usque ad Tigrim, est
Parthia *triginta tribus regionibus
distincta.* *Dicitur autem Parthia
a Parthis*...

Est in ea regio Aracusia,...
Est etiam in ea Assyria, ab Assur,
filio Sem, qui eam primus inco-
luit nominata.

Est in ea quoque Media,...In ea
etiam Persida...
In hac primum orta est ars
magica.

Persida lapidem pyrrhitem mittit,

qui manum prementis urit,...

°"De Tygrés...Idumian."
LIBER I. CAP. XV.—A Tigri
flumine usque ad Euphratem est
Mesopotamia,...

In hac est civitas Ninive,
itinere trium dierum,

---

[1] Cf. Hon., beginning of Cap. XI: "Deinde est India ab Indo flumine dicta.
Qui ad Septentrionem de monte Caucaso nascitur." [2] ke eg. (*sic*).
[3] De ceste...Tygris: Parthia, a large country, *extends* from this mountain which is
so large as far as the river Tigris. [4] Cf. ll. 246, 271. [5] Corr. *Assire*, cf.
l. 601 and Hon. "Assyria ab Assur." [6] Repeated as catchword. [7] Corr. *main.*
[8] Corr. *Tigris*, cf. ll. 246, 271, 597. [9] Corr. *est.* [10] Une (terre?) garnie.
[11] Corr. *de.* Or, perhaps, read "de terrure," *i.e.* territory. But, in the MS., *dec*
and *errure* are written very distinctly in two words.

625 Ninos ki l'estora
     Ninivé l'apela,
     E Mainrot, un geant
     Ke a merveilles fu grant,
     Si fist primerement
630 Des murs le fundement.
     .l. coutes sunt
     De lé les murs k'i sunt,
     E de haut unt .ii. c.c.
     Eufratés curt dedenz.
635 Mult li sunt li estre bel.
     La est la tour Babel.
     Sachez, n'est un gas,
     Ke .iiii. mile pas
     A cele tur de haut,
640 Si ke un sul n'ent fauut[1].
     Aprés si est Cardée.
     De iloec fu aporté
     Primes astrimonie:
p.416 Sachez,   ne vus   ment
          mie.
645 Aprés si est Arabe
     K'en puet apeler Sabe,
     Nomé par .ii. nouns
     Ke nomé vus avums.
     Li encens vent de la
650 K'en nus aporte sa :
     Issi sil awm prest.
     En Arabe si est
     Le mont de Synai,
     Celui de Orep hausi
655 Ou Deu la lai dona ;
     Moysen l'enseigna.
     En Arabe converse
     Mainte mult gent[2] diverse
     Ki unt a nun Amonite,
660 Li autre Moabite,
     Sarazin, Madian
     E li Idumian°.

a Nino rege constructa et nominata....Hanc Nemrod gigas fun-
davit ; *sed Semiramis regina repa-
ravit.*

Cujus muri latitudo est quinquaginta cubitorum,

altitudo ducentorum cubitorum,
...fluvio Euphrate per medium
ejus currente irrigua.
Hujus arx Babel,

quatuor millia passuum alta scribitur.

In ea quoque est Chaldaea, in
qua primum inventa est astro-
nomia.

In ea et Arabia, quae etiam Saba
dicitur, a Saba filio Chus.

In hac thus colligitur ;

in hac est mons Sina, qui et
Oreb,

in quo lex a Moyse scribitur
accepta ;...In ea sunt gentes
multae,
Moabitae, Ammonitae,

Idumaei, Sarraceni, Madianitae,
et aliae multae.

---

[1] Corr. *faut.*   [2] Corr. *gent mult,* but cf. l. 396.

Dreit est ke oiez aprés
De l'ewe de Eufratés
665 Decke a Mer Moienne
Ke mult nus est logtaine.
La s'estent, ceo oi dire,
La cuntré d'Isire[1];
Sirus li reis out nun.
670 Iloec si est Damas,
Més ne sai hout[2] ou bas,
Ou en plain ou en roche.
Aprés si est Antioche,
p. 417 Comagene e Fenice,
675 Une tere mult riche.
En cele tere la
Une oisel i a
Ke fenix a nun;
Pur li apele l'un
680 Fenice la cuntrée,
Veritez est prové.
Iloec est un mont *grans*,
La ou crest li libans;
Verités est e fine.
685 Aprest[3] Palestine
Ke tut pleinement sone
En noz tere Escaloigne.
Aprés si est Judé
Ke l'em nome Cananée;
690 Noun unt de Chanaan,
Celui ke fu fiz Cam;
Judée, pur Juda
Ke Jacob engendra.
La est, c'est veritez,
695 Jer*u*salem[4] la citez
Ke Seim le fiz Noé
Estrut en sun eé.
Kaunt Sem la comença,
De sun nun la noma
700 Salem, ceo sachet ben,
Mar douterez de ren.

, "Dreit est…l'avoit establie."
LIBER I. CAP. XVI.—Ab Euphrate
usque ad mare Mediterraneum

est Syria,

a quodam Syro rege dicta,
in qua est Damascus,…

Est in ea Comagena provincia.
Est et Phoenicia,
a Phoenice ave, quae sola in hac
terra invenitur,…

In hac etiam mons est Libanus,
*ad cujus radicem oritur Jordanis
fluvius.*
Est in ea quoque Palaestina, a
civitate Palaestin, quae nunc As-
calon vocatur, dicta.
Est in ea Judaea, a Juda filio
Jacob, *de cujus tribu reges erant,*
nuncupata. In hac etiam Chana-
naea a Chanaan filio Cham dicta.

In hac est Jerusalem,
quam Sem filius Noe construens,

Salem nominavit.

---

[1] Corr. *de Sire.* [2] Corr. *haut. Hout* may be, however, a form due to the influence of the Southern or Midland dialects. [3] Corr. *Aprés est.*
[4] Cf. *Jerosolime,* l. 714.

Aprés, ge n'i sai plus,
I fu Jebeseus   Sed Jebus,

p.418 Ki fu fiz Canaan;   et filius Chanaan inhabitavit,
705 S'i habita meinte an.   unde Jebus et Salem dedit ei
     De celui e de Sem   nomen rex David Jerusalem,
     Out noun Jer*usa*lem[1];   quasi Jebusalem.
     David si la noma
     Ki durement l'ama.

710 Salomon, fiz David,   Quam Salomon filius ejus auro
     La cité enbelit   et gemmis decoravit,
     De fin or e de argent.
     Noma la vereiment
     Tut dreit Jerosolime[2],   Jeroselyniam quasi Jerusalemo-
715 Si cum nus dit la rime.   niam appellavit.
     Més la degasterent,   Quam a Babyloniis subversam,
     Destruerent e praerent
     Li Babiloniën
     Ki le ne amoient ren.

720 Més pus Zorobabel   Zorobabel reaedificavit;
     La refist ben e bel.
     Pus cel tens, ce est la some,
     La destruit l'ost de Rome.   sed Romanus exercitus postea
     Més aprés poi de tens   funditus delevit.
725 Elius Adrians   Hanc postmodum Aelius Adri-
     Ki fu fort empere   anus imperator reparavit,
     E tint ben sun empire,
     Ben la renovela
     E fist. Si la noma
730 Pur Elius Elie,   Aeliamque nominavit.
     Kaunt l'[3] avoit establie*.
     Aprés cele cuntrée   *"Aprés cele cuntrée...en sa
     Ke *vus* ai divisé   manere."

p.419 S'estent, p*ar* maint repaire, LIBER I. CAP. XVII.—Est et in
735 Samarie, une tere   Palaestina regio Samaria, a civitate
     Ke ore noment la gent   Samaria dicta,
     Sabaste pleinement.   quae nunc Sebastia est nuncupata
     Galilé aprés chet,   ...In hac est quoque Galilaea, in
     La ou Nazareth siet,   qua est Nazareth civitas,
740 Riche de argent e de or,
     Lez le mont de Tabor.   juxta montem Thabor sita.

[1] Cf. *Jerosolime*, l. 714.   [2] Cf. ll. 695, 707.   [3] *l* above the line.

La outre en Galilée
Ki grant tere est e lée
Si a la une pais
745 Ke a noun Pentapolis.
Une poumes la sunt
Ke si *grant* beauté unt
Ke pur desirer
De ces poumes mang*er*
750 Engendrent la gent :
Si n'en dotez nent.
S'en le¹ touche pur prendre
Taunt tost devenent cendre ;
si sunt de cele manere
755 K'eles rendent fumere².
Aprés cele cuntrée
Si s'estent Nabacée,
Une issi dite tere.
Bon est en sa manere⁷.
760 Aprés est Egypte
Ke n'est mie petite.
Thebaide aprés vent
Ke mult de tere tent⁷.
p.420 De Scape³, une mer gent
765 Ki curt en orient,
Si vet par maint endreit
Vers Europe dreit,
Caucasus, une mont grant.
Iloec sunt habitant
770 Fenmes, ben set l'um,
Amazones unt nun ;
Vertu unt fort e grant,
Cum hommes cumbatant.
Serés est un chasteaus
775 Utre orient, mult beaus,
Dunt Serice est nomé,
Une riche cuntrée.
Aprés si est un autre
Ke l'en apele Bautre.

In hac est et Pentapolis regio, ...

Isid., *Etym.* XIV, iii, 24–5.
"24. Pentapolis regio in confinio
Arabiae et Palaestinae sita....
25. Cujus umbra quaedam, et
species in favillis, et arboribus
ipsis etiam adhuc videtur. Nas-
cuntur enim ibi poma virentia
sub tanta specie maturitatis, ut
edendi desiderium gignant.
Si carpas, fatiscunt, ac resolvuntur
in cinerem, fumumque exhalant,
quasi adhuc ardeant."

Honor. LIB. I. CAP. XVII.—...In
hac et Nabathaei...

⁵"Aprés est Egypte...tent."
LIBER I. CAP. XVIII.—...Haec
prius et Bona copia...Aegyptus
est vocata....
...In hac est provincia Thebaida.
⁷"De Scape...en vie."
LIBER I. CAP. XIX.—...Mons
Caucasus a Caspio mari orientis
attollitur, et per Aquilonem ver-
gens pene usque ad Europam
porrigitur. Hunc inhabitabant
Amazones feminae videlicet ut
viri proeliantes....

...Seres est oppidum Orientis,
quo Serica regio,...est dicta.

Post hanc est Bactra, *a Bactro
amne vocata.*

---

¹ Corr. *les.*   ² Une poumes...fumere: This passage, which is wanting in
Honorius, is clearly borrowed from Isidorus.   ³ Corr. *De Caspe*, cf. l. 323 and
Hon. "a Caspio mari."

780   A cele, ke home die,
Si ceo[1] joint Hircanie,
Un tere mult clere;
De bestes est plenere.
En cere tere la
785   Mult tresgrant bois i a;
Oisel i sunt manaunt
Ki par nuit[2] lusant.
Aprés est Site e Hune,
Mult est large checune.
790   Albanie aprés vent;
Armenie a le tent.
En Armanie est un monz,
Attarat est si nounz.

p.421   Iloec remest e sit
795   Le arche ke Noé fit
Pus le deluuge[3] assez,
Pus ke il fu trespassez.
Ibere est iloec prés
E Capadoce aprés.
800   Les yves la conceivent
Del vent ke eles receivent.
Lur fons ne sunt mie
Plus de .iiij. ans en vie'.
Lez la tere ke ai dite
805   Si est Asie la Petite.
Une mer la purprent,
Tant cum ele s'etent.
La est, ce est verité,
Ephesus, la cité;
810   Grant est e tele non a;
Sein Jon si gist la,
Li bon ewangelistres
Ki fu li Deu ministres.
Aprés Asie la Meindre
815   Poez Bitine prendre[v].
Juste li est asis
Galatie e pus Frise.
Dardane est lez celi,
E Ysaure autresi.

Huic conjungitur Hyrcania,
Isid., *Etym.* xiv, iii, 33.
"Hyrcania…Est autem silvis aspera, copiosa immanibus feris, tigribus, pantherisque ac pardis."
Hon. Liber I. Cap. XIX.…ab Hyrcana sylva nominata, in qua sunt aves quarum pennae splendent per noctes. Huic jungitur Scythia et Hirnia,
…Hanc sequitur Albania,…
…Cui connectitur Armenia, in qua est mons Arath,

super quem arca Noe post diluvium requievit,…

…Huic copulatur Iberia.
Illi vero Cappadocia,…
in hac equae a vento concipiunt,

sed foetus non amplius triennio vivunt.
[u]"Lez la tere…prendre."
Liber I. Cap. XX.—Asia Minor post hanc constituitur quae pene undique mari cingitur.
In hac est Ephesus civitas,…

in qua requiescit corpus Joannis Evangelistae;…

…Prima provincia Asiae Minoris est Bithynia,…
[v]"Juste li…est nomé."
Liber I. Cap. XXI.—…Huic jungitur Galatia,…Hanc sequitur Phrygia,…Haec et Dardania…

---

[1] Corr. *se.*   [2] Corr. *par nuit sunt luisant.*   [3] Corr. *deluge.*

820 Aprés est ajustée
    Cilice, une cuntrée.
    La ci est une cité,
    Tharse, ceo est verité.

Deinde est Isauria,
…Post hanc est Cilicia,…
…In hac et Tharsus civitas,…

p.422 Mult delitable esteit
825 Kaunt Sein Pol i maneit.

Pauli apostoli inhabitatione glori-
osa.

    En aprés ces cuntrées
    Ke[1] *vus* ai devisées
    Si est Lice veirement,
    E Pamphile ensement.

Deinde est Lycia…
et Pamphylia…

830 En Lice est un mont
        grant
    Ke par nuit est ardaunt ;
    Grant est e haut e lez,
    Cimere est apelez.

Isid., *Etym.* xiv, iii, 46.
"Lycia nuncupata,…Ibi est mons
Chimoera, qui nocturnis aestibus
ignem exhalat, sicut in Sicilia
Aetna, et Vesuvius in Campania."

    Del mund aveth oie
835 La primere partie
    Ki est Asie apelé,

Hon. LIBER I. CAP. XXI.…Post
decursam Asiam,

    Cum ele est grant e lé,
    E cum ele set e va,
    E quele teres i a.
840 Ore est dreit e sens,

transeamus ad Europam.

    Si l'aporte resuns[2],
    Ke *vus* oiez imés
    De la secunde aprés
    Ke Europe est nomé[v].
845 Ben *vus* iert devisé.
    Teres i ad *grant* masse :

[w]"Teres i ad…ovec."
LIBER I. CAP. XXIII.—A Thanai

    Sisse ke plus est basse,
    Si s'estent vers meidi
    Del fluie de Thanai
850 Deske Dismon, le flueve,
    Si cum v*er*ité le preve.

fluvio est Scythia inferior,
quae versus meridiem usque
ad Danubium porrigitur.

    Alanie rest iluec,
    Gocie e Dace ovec[w].

In hac sunt istae provinciae,
Alania, Dacia, Gothia.

p.423 Pus Dimon est durant
855 Ermenie[3] le Grant.

[x]"Pus Dimon…cuntré."
LIBER I. CAP. XXIV.—A Danu-

    A lui est ajusté
    Soueve, une cuntré[x].

bio…est Germania superior…
In hac est regio Suevia,…

---

[1] Ke ķ (*sic*).   [2] The rhyme *sens* : *resuns*, although resting on a mere con-
sonance, does not seem to call for an emendation.   [3] Corr. *Germenie*. Cf. l. 859
and Hon. "Germania."

E aprés poeth prendre
Armenie[1] la Meindre.
860 E[2] aprés establie
La tere de Messie,
E Pannomie e Trace[y].
Ke cil tenent d'espace
Grece e Damacie[3],
865 Molesse e Caonie.
Aprés ceo est Hylaide,
Thessaile e Chaide[4].
Lez cest[5] tenanz
Istre, une tere granz[z].
870 Italle aprés chet,
U Tusce, une pais, siet,
E Apuille e Hungrie[6],
E aprés Lumbardie,
E pus Venice e France,
875 Ce sachet, sanz dotance,
Aquitaine e Espaine
E Gascoine[7] e Britaine,
Engletere, e Hyberne
Ou plus de l'an yverne.
880 Outre icele cuntrée
Si est la mer[8] gelée.
De Europe awm dit
E mustré e descrit,
p. 424 Des teres, des cuntrées,
885 Cum eles sunt posées,
Si cum verité l'afiche.
Ore parlerum de Aufrike
Ki content, par esgart,
De la mund la terce
part[9a].
890 La primere cuntrée
Si est Libe nomé;
Pus Cyienaiche,
Une tere mult riche,

[y] "E aprés... Trace."
LIBER I. CAP. XXV.—Ab Albia
fluvio est Germania inferior...A
Danubio, usque ad mare Mediter-
raneum est Messias...deinde Pan-
nonia... [Thracia,...
LIBER I. CAP. XXVI.—Inde
[z] "Ke cil...granz."
LIBER I. CAP. XXVII.—...est
Graecia,... Dalmatia... Est et
Chaonia,...Haec et Molosia...Est
ibi et Elladia,...Ibi et Thessalia
...Ibi est Achaia...Ibi et Arcadia
...Deinde est Pannonia superior
usque ad Peninum montem. Ad
aquilonem ejus Histria, ...
[a] "Italle...terce part."
LIBER I. CAP. XXVIII.—Italia...
Est in Italia Tuscia provincia,...
Ibi est et Apulia. Est et Imbria,...
Est et Longobardia...Venetia...
Gallia...
LIBER I. CAP. XXIX.—...Haec
et Francia...Aquitaniam...
LIBER I. CAP. XXX.—Inde est
Hispania...
LIBER I. CAP. XXXI.—...Britan-
nia, Anglia, Hibernia,...Chile...
in qua sex mensibus, videlicet
aestivis est continuus dies, sex
hibernis continua nox.
Ultra hanc versus aquilonem
est mare congelatum,...
Europam perambulavimus.
Ad Africam transmigremus.
[b] "La primere...lontaigne."
LIBER I. CAP. XXXII.—Africa
...Hujus prima provincia est
Libya,...Inde est Cyrenaica...

---

[1] Corr. *Germenie*. Cf. l. 855 and Hon. "Germania." [2] =est. [3] Ke cil...
Damacie G.=As much space as the former do Greece etc. occupy. [4] Chaide:
Arcadia, *or* Achaia. [5] ?Corr. *Lez celi est tenanz*. Cf. l. 818. [6] Cf. Hon.
Imbria, ? read Himgrie. [7] Cf. Isid., *Etym.* IX, ii, 107. [8] mere̜ (*sic*), cf. l. 207.
[9] Cf. l. 189 and Hon. *De Im. Mundi* I, vii.

Bisicene[1], e Zeucheis[2]	Post hanc Bisace,...deinde est
895 Ke mult est grant pais.	Heusis, in qua est magna Car-
La est la grant Cartage	thago...
Ou a maint herbergage.	
Aprés est establie	
Cetule e Numidie.	Post hanc est Getulia. Inde
900 Aprés est Moletaigne,	Numidia,...Inde est Mauritania.
Une tere lontaigne[b].	
De Ethiope vus di	'"De Ethiope...environ."
Ke ele est vers medi.	LIBER I. CAP. XXXIII.—Versus
Cele part sunt manant	meridiem vero est Aethiopia,...
905 Une gent Garmant.	Inter quas sunt Garamantes,...
En cele tere la	
Une fontaigne i a	Apud quos est fons tam frigidus
Ki est freid par jur,	diebus,
E nul, pur la freidur,	
910 Ne poet prendre ne beivre,	ut non bibatur;
Pur veirs le poet creire;	
E par nuit ensement	tam fervidus noctibus,
Si tresgrant chalur rent	
p.425 Ke n'i poet adeser	ut non tangatur.
915 Ne beivre ne guster.	
Outre, vers orient,	Quibus versus orientem
Sunt manant une gent,	cohabitant
Tragodite apelé,	Troglodytae,
Ki, par igneleté,	qui celeri cursu
920 Vont les bestes sauvages	feras capiunt....
Prendre par les boscages.	
Outre la fin de Aufrike	In extremis finibus Africae...
Ad une cité riche.	est urbs Gades,...
Noble est e grant e lé;	
925 Gadres est apelé.	
Mer ki Gadite a non	de qua Gaditanum mare
La porçaint environ[c].	dicitur.
Ore awm acumplies	
Del mund les treis parties.	
930 Dist vus avum levement	
Tut le establement	

[1] B' (sic); cf. Isid., Etym. XIV, v, 7, Byzacena regio...   [2] i above the line;
cf. Isid., Etym. XV, v, 8, Zeugis, ubi Carthago magna...

Del mund, e queus i est.
Grant preu e grant *cum-*
quest[1]
Receivre il purrount
935 Cil ki ben entendrount.

---

[1] This, the only instance of the abbreviation 9, has been expanded as *cum* on account of l. 336, where "cumquist" is written in full.

INDEX OF PROPER NAMES

[1] Cf. K. Miller, *Mappaemundi*, t. VI (Stuttgart 1895).

[1] K. Miller, o.c., vol. VI.

VOCABULARY

(**A** = Poem on the Assumption. **B** = Day of Judgment. **C** = Divisiones Mundi.)

abuns, C 77, see aubes
acerter, A 26, 190, 218: to assure, show the truth
acorent, C 484: they kill
acorsez, C 457: swift
adeissent, C 356: they touch
afiche, C 190, 886: declares, affirms
afornent, C 408: they bake
ajustée, C 820, 856: placed next
alloine, C 466: breath
aluer, A 195, 216: to place
angules, C 559: eel
aparcevent, A 56: visibly
aparilé, A 159: ready
arbreilles, C 372: bushes
aseint, C 85: surrounds
asmé, A 160: disposed
astrimonie, C 643: astronomy
atemprement, C 122: moderation
aubes, C 56; abuns, C 77; aubuns, C 86: white of egg
s'avauncent, C 402: advance

beuz, C 336: fair things
bloi, C 511; 'fulvi,' tawny
burkes, C 291: towns
busines, B 85: trumpets

ceinte, C 178: circuit
cha, A 205: hither
cheir, A 308: to fall
contretrové, A 236: invented
contrevement, A 234: invention
corsue, C 498: stout, corpulent
corvés, C 425: curved
cotes, C 386, 565; cothes, C 362; coutes, C 631: cubit
cowe, C 503, etc.: tail
crié, A 40, 346: created
cumpassez, C 170: arranged
cuniseit, A 322: knew
cuntendreit, A 256: would behave
cunverser, A 61, 288; C 657: to dwell

deck, C 12; decke, C 597, 665; dekes, C 198; deske, C 516, 850, A 36, 298; dreske, C 195: until
delivre (a), C 351; in peace
desertines, C 281: desert places
deskevre, C 2: discovers
desturnant, A 19: to turn to and fro, over and over

desvéement, A 235: a mad thing
divisiun, C 489: division, part

ef, C 49, 53, 61, etc.: egg
el, A 205: any other thing
emfassez, C 113: envelope
s'empaint, C 265: 'labitur,' flows away
enfomente, C 611: bewitches
enorte, C 42: teaches
enumbré, A 161: innumerable
envaie, C 35: undertaken
enveillez, C 407: old
eprist, A 183, for enprist, with fall of A.N. *n*: began
errure, C 623, see note
escaille, C 68; eskale, C 54, 55: egg-shell
espont, C 249: expounds
establement, C 931: establishment
estora, C 625; estoré, A 151: to construct, build
estre, C 635: the plan
estreit, A 334: strictly
estrut, C 697: built
estué, A 35: hidden, put away
estuerre, C 579: (for "estordre") to drag away
evillissent, C 367: they grow old
evre, C 1: work
ewangelistres, C 812: evangelist

ferment, C 8: strongly
fie, fiez, A 23, 312; C 180: time, occasion
flueve, C 850; fluies, C 238, etc.; fluvies, C 241: river
fons, C 802: foal
froncist, C 380: wrinkles
fumere, C 755: smoke
fundé, C 6; foundé, C 9: learned

germeine, C 61: germ
grant, A 9: desire

hantent, C 441: dwell
hardement, A 324: boldness
heire, B 61: hair shirt
heitez, B 24: merry
herbergage, C 897: lodging

idle, C 288: island

igneleté, C 919: swiftness
imés, C 842: now (=huimés)

jou, B 58: game
jovenesce, C 404: youth
juisse, B 73: judgment
just, C 257, 816: next
justise, B 74: judge
juvence, C 368: youth

ke, k', A 48, 52, etc.; C 84, 187, etc.: relative and interrogative pronoun, nom. form
ki, A 255; C 432: conjunction; A 346; C 147, 150: relative pronoun, acc. form

la, A 117 (de si la): henceforward
lé, C 632: breadth
leiser, B 58: to leave
limaçon, C 571: 'testudo,' tortoise
loé, A 91: advised

menvers, C 513: mottled?
més, B 42 (le mes): all the more
moel, C 87; moels, C 93; moiels, C 58, 59: yolk of egg
moiste, C 130: wet
moistez, C 127: wetness
mostrement, C 101 (faire mostrement): to show
mund, C 3, 44, 47: world
mund, C 324, 325, 330: mountain
muntant, C 308: amount
muscez, A 227: hidden

neseit, B 8: naistre, to be born, or naiser, to mortify

ordeinement, C 102: order
oreit, A 255: would hear
orteus, C 421: toes
ovelement, C 140: equally

par+adj., C 466: very
parais, C 212: paradise
peigne, B 76: pain
perite, C 614: pyrite
pevre, C 370, 379: pepper
porçaint, C 927; porcent, C 69: surrounds

porté, C 46: contents
postive, B 56 (seit postive): has power
poucinet, C 97: chicken
praerent, C 717: they despoiled
prestement, B 137: permission
privé, A 114, 281: intimate, confidential
provement, C 168: proof

quereler, A 187: to discuss
quire, C 339: to cook
quirunt, C 339: they will seek to, try to
quises, C 490: thighs

refectiun, A 175: comfort
rendu, A 71: taken the veil
rensoili, B 90: soiled
resemblable, C 218: like
respunt, C 506: 'reflectit,' turns back
retraire (sanz...), C 409: without hesitation
retreit, A 266: related

sach, B 61: bag
sauvagines, C 282: wild beasts
secks, C 123: dry
sifle, C 531: hissing
sumoila, A 128: slumbered
sumus, A 343: we are

teste, C 572: shell, (see note)
touche, C 466: sweet (par+touch: very sweet)
treche, B 58: dance

utime, A 72: eighth
uverant, A 15: to exercise
uveré, A 135: disposed

veire, B 62: variegated
vengance, B 126: reward
vermesel, C 563: worm
verseiller, B 48: to sing
vertist, C 379: changes
vesché, A 52: bishopric, diocese
virounez, C 54: surrounded
visablement, A 242: visibly
vut, A 321: face

yves, C 800: mares